"This book is a great asset for org___ involved in autism at work emplc___ some of the challenges that peop___ workplace and provides managers with strategies to deal with those challenges. It is a must-read for any organization embarking on the neuro-diversity journey."

—*Michael Fieldhouse, Dandelion Program Executive, DXC Technology, Adjunct Professor Cyber Security, La Trobe University*

"*An Employer's Guide to Managing Professionals on the Autism Spectrum* stands out for its comprehensive and contemporary presentation of information. Its delivery of crisp situational guidance makes it unique and especially useful in today's competitive landscape, where employers are looking to tap into this unexplored talent pool. I highly recommend this book to be read not just once, but to be at the ready for managers to create a strong work environment and elicit great performance from those who are on the spectrum."

—*James Mahoney, Executive Director and Head of Autism at Work, JP Morgan Chase & Company*

"This book offers an accessible and clear overview for supervisors, co-workers, and individuals on the autism spectrum about how to improve the employment experience for professionals with autism. It provides a useful look at why there is increased interest in improving employment outcomes for this group, potential issues to anticipate, and ways to improve the likelihood of a successful job match and improved outcomes in retention and advancement over time."

—*Susanne M. Bruyere, Director, K. Lisa Yang and Hock E. Tan Institute for Employment and Disability, Cornell University ILR School*

**In memory of
WILLIAM "SAM" KOWALSKY
and
DOROTHY S. KOWALSKY**

"Marcia Scheiner and Joan Bogden's excellent book is a very valuable guide to the challenges that people with autism face in the workplace, balanced with the assets and gifts that they bring to the workplace. Employers and fellow employees will find their book highly readable and helpful in knowing how to accommodate a colleague with autism, acknowledging their disability (which can often be misunderstood), and coming up with ways to make reasonable adjustments for them. In doing so, this will help ensure the workplace is inclusive for people with autism. In turn, the employer will benefit from the talents in people with autism, in excellent attention to detail, perfectionism, going the extra mile, and innovative ways of looking at information."

—*Professor Simon Baron-Cohen, Director,*
Autism Research Centre, Cambridge University

AN EMPLOYER'S GUIDE TO MANAGING PROFESSIONALS ON THE AUTISM SPECTRUM

of related interest

Autism Equality in the Workplace
Removing Barriers and Challenging Discrimination
Janine Booth
Foreword by John McDonnell MP
ISBN 978 1 84905 678 6
eISBN 978 1 78450 197 6

Business for Aspies
42 Best Practices for Using Asperger Syndrome
Traits at Work Successfully
Ashley Stanford
ISBN 978 1 84905 845 2
eISBN 978 0 85700 501 4

Asperger Syndrome and Employment
What People with Asperger Syndrome Really Really Want
Sarah Hendrickx
ISBN 978 1 84310 677 7
eISBN 978 1 84642 879 1

Helping Adults with Asperger's Syndrome Get & Stay Hired
Career Coaching Strategies for Professionals and
Parents of Adults on the Autism Spectrum
Barbara Bissonnette
ISBN 978 1 84905 754 7
eISBN 978 1 78450 052 8

AN EMPLOYER'S GUIDE TO MANAGING PROFESSIONALS ON THE AUTISM SPECTRUM

Marcia Scheiner, Integrate Autism Employment Advisors
with Joan Bogden *Illustrations by Meron Philo*

Jessica Kingsley *Publishers*
London and Philadelphia

First published in 2017
by Jessica Kingsley Publishers
73 Collier Street
London N1 9BE, UK
and
400 Market Street, Suite 400
Philadelphia, PA 19106, USA

www.jkp.com

Library of Congress Cataloging in Publication Data
A CIP catalog record for this book is available from the Library of Congress

British Library Cataloguing in Publication Data
A CIP catalogue record for this book is available from the British Library

ISBN 978 1 78592 745 4
eISBN 978 1 78450 513 4

Printed and bound in the United States

This book is dedicated to all the women and men on the autism spectrum who struggle every day to find and keep appropriate employment.

CONTENTS

ACKNOWLEDGMENTS

Integrate Autism Employment Advisors (formerly known as the Asperger Syndrome Training & Employment Partnership: ASTEP) was founded in 2010 to increase inclusive competitive employment opportunities for college graduates with autism. We do this by helping organizations identify, recruit, and retain qualified professionals on the autism spectrum, and we are a leader in employer-focused solutions for the inclusion of college graduates with autism in competitive employment.

Integrate brings a unique understanding of both our clients and job candidates through our corporate and personal experience. We are experts in creating corporate engagement, sourcing qualified candidates, and connecting the two. It is the work of the past six years that has provided us with the experience to write this book, which we hope will not only guide employers in being successful managers and colleagues of professionals on the autism spectrum, but will also provide more opportunities for professionals with autism to flourish in the work environment of their choice.

We could not have written this book without the many individuals on the spectrum who shared their personal experiences with us over the years. In particular, I want to thank James G., Peter R., Karl W., Bill F., and Eric K. for sharing their personal stories with us in our early years. While too many to name, I want to thank the many young adults who have participated in our Employer Connect and Job Search Boot Camp programs for providing us with the insights into how you are all uniquely talented individuals that have so much to offer an employer. I also want to thank Michael John Carley who, as Integrate's Executive Director from 2011 to 2014, not only shared his own experiences with us, but was instrumental in helping Integrate launch. Over the years we have received professional guidance from Dr. Lynda Geller and Dr. Brenda Smith Myles. Their experience and depth of knowledge through working with adults on the autism spectrum continues to be an invaluable guide for us not only in writing this book, but also in our daily activities.

I also want to thank the many employers we have met who have openly discussed their desire to include neuro-diverse individuals in their workplace, and to make sure they are providing a supportive work environment for these employees. One of our earliest supporters, PwC, deserves special mention not only for their efforts to incorporate neuro-diversity in their workplace, but also for their efforts in supporting Integrate's work more broadly. I'd also like to thank the over thirty corporations who have hosted the young adults participating in our Employer Connect program—Barclays, Cisco, Disney, The Economist, EY, KIND Snacks, LinkedIn, Merck, and PwC among them. Watching the interaction of the young adult participants in our program and these employers has taught us many lessons, which we share in this book.

A project like this takes the efforts and support of many people to come to fruition. This book could not have been written without the dedicated work of Tracy Powell-Rudy and Harrison Potasnik, Integrate's Director of Corporate Development and Program Manager, respectively. Tracy's tireless efforts in engaging employers in our work and running our Job Search Boot Camp program has provided us with the vast experience in how to support professionals with autism in the workplace shared in the book. Tracy and Harrison provide a significant portion of the collective memory of Integrate and helped brainstorm the topics and issues that needed to be covered in this book. Along with Amy Conn, Integrate's Director of Marketing and West Coast Representative, they were also eagle-eyed proofreaders. As with any project, funding support is always critical. I would like to acknowledge the MJS Foundation for their continuous support of Integrate. It has been enormously helpful in allowing this book to come to completion. I also want to thank my co-author Joan Bogden and our illustrator Meron Philo. Joan was not only an author, editor, and researcher; she kept this project organized and focused. This book would not have gotten written without her. Meron is a young artist whose artwork in this book is just the tip of his artistic abilities.

Lastly, I want to thank my son. Were it not for him, I never would have started Integrate and written this book. And aside from being his mother, pursuing the work of Integrate is the most rewarding thing I have ever done.

Marcia Scheiner

Part One

INTRODUCTION

Numerous books have been written on the art and science of management. While being a good manager is as much an art as it is a science, when working with individuals who have a neuro-diverse profile, managers need to have a different level of understanding. Most of the managers we meet are busy people who want quick, clear advice on solving problems. They want concrete solutions for specific issues that they can apply in a relatively short period of time.

In this book we have set out to combine the art and science of managing professionals on the autism spectrum with concrete advice for addressing specific situations that may arise in the workplace when managing or working with these individuals. Throughout we provide explanations for what drives the behavioral differences of your colleagues on the autism spectrum. These first three chapters will help increase your understanding of why it is important to be knowledgeable about autism in the workplace.

Chapter 1

GETTING STARTED

Today, 35% of young adults with an autism spectrum diagnosis are attending college. If they can get a college degree, why can't they find a job?

Since the Centers for Disease Control and Prevention (CDC) reported that the incidence rate of autism among children was 1 in 166 in 2000, the scientific community has been debating whether or not the US is suffering from an autism epidemic. The incidence rate of autism has climbed four times since then, to where it rests today at 1 in 68. Epidemic or not, the fact remains that every year thousands of 18-year-olds with autism transition into adulthood with the same hopes and aspirations as their non-autistic (or *neuro-typical*) peers—employment, a safe home, and nurturing relationships. Yet today, young adults with autism experience the highest unemployment rates of any group of individuals with disabilities.

In his research, Dr. Paul Shattuck of Drexel University found that two thirds of high school graduates on the autism spectrum have not experienced any form of employment within the first two years out of school. By the time they are in their twenties, only 58% of young adults with autism had some form of paid employment, compared to 74% of young adults with intellectual disabilities, 91% with a speech impairment or emotional disturbance, and 95% with a learning disability.[1]

While the increasing diagnosis rate and low employment rate for individuals with autism paint a grim picture, one statistic stood out as promising in Dr. Shattuck's research: today, 35% of young adults with an autism spectrum disorder (ASD) are attending college.[2, 3] Overall, however, many college-educated young adults diagnosed with an ASD are not finding employment upon graduation from college or are employed below their level of education. Anecdotal evidence from the autism community suggests that the unemployment rate of college graduates on the autism spectrum may be closer to 75–85%. These seemingly contradictory statistics raise two questions. How are over one third of today's young adults with autism able to complete post-secondary education? And if they can get a college degree, why can't they find a job?

To answer these questions, one needs to understand some of the history of autism diagnoses. When first recognized as a brain disorder in 1908, autism was considered a subset of schizophrenia. In 1980, autism was removed as a schizophrenia diagnosis and listed in the Diagnostic and Statistical Manual of Mental Disorders (DSM) as a separate condition. In 1994, *Asperger Syndrome* was added to the DSM, as an expansion of the definition of autism, to differentiate those individuals who had more advanced language development and normal to superior IQs, but still exhibited some of the other characteristics of autism, including social awkwardness, sensitivity to environmental stimuli (noise, light, and foods), unusual speech patterns, and repetitive behaviors. In 2014, the DSM was updated again, and Asperger Syndrome was folded into a broader definition of autism spectrum disorder and eliminated as a stand-alone diagnosis,[4] although the term Asperger Syndrome is still used by many people to distinguish where on the autism spectrum certain individuals fall. In this book, we mostly use the term *autism*, but occasionally use *Asperger Syndrome*, as many of the individuals holding professional-level jobs that we meet still identify with this term.

As the focus on autism as a separate condition from other brain disorders grew during the late 20th century, so did the focus on early diagnosis and intervention. According to the

CDC, a reliable diagnosis of autism can now be made at the age of two.[5] With children being diagnosed at very early ages, programs have developed that begin providing supports to children as young as 12 months old. In a study conducted in 2009 of a program called the Early Start Denver Model, it was found that early intervention "for very young children with autism…is effective for improving IQ, language ability, and social interaction."[6]

As children with autism receive greater levels of intervention and support, their ability to achieve higher levels of academic and social success has grown. Dr. Shattuck's finding that over one third of 18-year-olds with an ASD go on to college is proof of the success of early intervention and childhood supports. Today, a number of colleges and universities throughout the U.S. have such a significant population of students on the autism spectrum that they have created specialized support programs for their autistic students, separate from their traditional disability services offices. Many even market these programs to the autism community to attract and retain students on the spectrum.

But support for individuals on the autism spectrum who have completed college often stops when they graduate. The U.S. state-based vocational services model has not proven itself adept at finding competitive employment for the computer programmer, journalist, accountant, or graphic designer whose disability is related to his challenges with socialization and communication. Increased support through college, lagging vocational support services, and lack of employer understanding together result in the high unemployment rate among college graduates with autism.

Employers are just beginning to understand that having autism and being a successful professional are not mutually exclusive. It is important for employers who want to access this untapped talent pool to understand that the road to successful employment for college graduates on the autism spectrum is a two-way street. While employers look for candidates who "fit" into their corporate culture, employers must also provide an environment that guides individuals who are neuro-diverse on how to "fit" in. *Integrate* (formerly known as ASTEP, the Asperger Syndrome Training & Employment Partnership Inc.) was founded in 2010 to work with employers to change this dynamic for professionals on the autism spectrum. We see this as the logical next step in supporting such individuals so that they can be successful job seekers and employees.

This book is meant to provide you (as a manager, mentor, co-worker or HR professional) with concrete tools to understand and help guide your colleagues on the spectrum through the daily challenges they may experience on the job. Although this book focuses primarily on the *challenges* that may arise in the workplace when an employee has an autism spectrum disorder, these individuals prove to be loyal, honest, hardworking, focused, intelligent, accurate, logical, and productive. For every challenging characteristic of being on the spectrum, one can find a positive use of that trait over a wide range of jobs. For example, what employer wouldn't want a risk manager who is exceptionally honest, a financial analyst who is obsessed with accuracy, a computer programmer who is laser-focused, or a graphic designer who is unconcerned with prior convention? And above all, who wouldn't want an employee who is grateful for an opportunity to have meaningful, competitive employment in an environment where they know they can be themselves and have their work valued?

How to use this book

Most managers, when dealing with an employee-relations issue, want a solution for the issue at hand, so that the problem can be fixed and everyone can move on with their busy day. It is the rare individual who has time to sit and read an entire book, or watch a lengthy training video, to learn about the different behaviors they encounter at work and how to manage them successfully. With that in mind, this book is written to provide managers and colleagues of individuals on the spectrum with targeted advice on how to understand, manage and get the best out of their employees on the autism spectrum, specifically those in *high-skill* or *professional-level* positions.

Each chapter in this book is written to address a particular challenge a professional with autism may have, and how it may present in the workplace. We start by providing examples of the behaviors you may see in the work environment that relate to both the challenge area and being on the autism spectrum, followed by an explanation of the underlying issues as to why this behavior is occurring. We then provide a description of how to deal with these behaviors in a respectful and effective manner. Lastly, as many of the behaviors resulting from autism may have their roots in more than one area of challenge, we provide references to other chapters that might provide additional information on the particular behavior in question, and close with a summary of the management strategies for the related behaviors.

Almost all the accommodations and management strategies that we recommend for working with professionals on the autism spectrum depend on *understanding why* these employees engage in certain behaviors. This information is an important factor in successfully implementing those strategies and accommodations and is provided in the main text of each chapter. While you might be tempted to jump straight to the chapter summaries, we strongly recommend that you read the material in the chapter(s) related to the behavior(s) you are seeing.

Throughout the book are quotes from professionals with autism/Asperger Syndrome that we interviewed who have learned to deal successfully with the challenges of the workplace—their perspectives provide not only additional strategies that they have used, but also a glimpse into the experience of being on the spectrum.

As you read this book, you will notice that we use the pronoun *he*, rather than *she*, throughout. Diagnosis rates for males on the autism spectrum far outweigh those for females. Whether this is due to men being affected with more frequency than women, or women being under-diagnosed, is up for debate. Regardless of the cause, we have chosen to use *he* for consistency in reading and not to imply that you will not encounter female co-workers on the autism spectrum.

Next steps

We suggest you read Chapter 2: The Autistic Professional in its entirety, as it will provide you with an overview of autism and why this is an important topic for all working individuals. After the introductory chapters in Part One, Chapters 4 to 13 are grouped into three main parts—Social Issues at Work, Work Performance, and Sensory Challenges—each of which includes the numbered sections that list examples of relevant behaviors. By referencing the table of contents, you should be able to turn quickly to the behavior or issue that most interests you and read why an employee is engaging in this behavior and how to properly manage or accommodate it, so the employee can be a successful part of your team.

As a reference guide, this book is designed to help you be a successful manager or colleague of individuals who exhibit certain styles of communication, ways of thinking, and physical behaviors generally associated with Asperger Syndrome and similar autism spectrum profiles. It is not meant as a means for diagnosis, and certainly some of these issues are not restricted to individuals on the autism spectrum. We hope this book will help you recognize some of the challenges that individuals with autism, particularly professionals, face in the workplace and learn how to respond to those challenges effectively. We also hope you will learn to identify and utilize the special skills and talents these individuals bring to the job to create a successful work experience for all involved.

Chapter 2

THE AUTISTIC PROFESSIONAL

You pass a colleague in the hallway on Monday morning, and in response to your polite, but somewhat rhetorical, question of "Hey, what'd you do this weekend?" he spends the next 20 minutes retelling the plot of the movie he saw without taking a breath. When done, he turns and walks away.

During a team meeting, while your boss is outlining a new project for your group, the person next to you is rocking back and forth on the back legs of his chair. When your boss asks for comments, he noisily drops his chair to the floor and says "You have structured this all wrong, so this project isn't worth doing." The room is drowning in silence.

You have taken on a new role as team leader. In your introduction to your team you tell them you have an "open door" policy and that everyone should feel free to come talk to you at any time. One of your team members shows up at your office multiple times a day and walks in talking, even when your door is closed.

Most everyone who has held a job has come across a colleague who just doesn't seem to fit in. They continually do things that make them stand out from their peers in the way they communicate and interact with others. They may talk too much, talk too loudly, or not talk at all. They may correct everyone, even for the smallest mistakes, yet never be able to admit they are wrong. They may be part of a team, but never greet any of their teammates in the hallway. Or they may appear to be on the verge of a meltdown every time you ask them to do something new. While working with colleagues like this can be frustrating, these same individuals can be exceptionally qualified in their area of expertise and innovative in their approach to solving problems.

An individual who struggles to fit in to the workplace, but excels at the job, may be struggling with issues related to having a neuro-diverse profile. *Neuro-diversity* is a term used to describe conditions like autism, dyslexia, and ADHD, and is meant to shift the focus of discourse about atypical ways of thinking and learning away from the usual litany of deficits, disorders, and impairments. The growth of conditions such as autism, combined with the increased focus on diversity and inclusion in the workplace, is resulting in a multitude of communication and working styles in the office. In this chapter, we will introduce you to autism in the workplace and the benefits for employers of hiring individuals on the autism spectrum.

Autism in the workplace

Autism is a *neurological* condition. The brains of individuals with autism are wired differently, resulting in sensory sensitivities, repetitive routines, intense focus on narrow areas of interest, and an inability to read social cues the way the rest of the world does. Colleagues often "interpret" these behaviors as rude, impolite, annoying, or just plain "odd" and assume that they are under the individual's control. Individuals with an autism spectrum disorder oftentimes use the term *neuro-typical* to describe people who are not on the autism spectrum. Perhaps you have noticed a colleague with some of these behaviors (see Table 2.1).

Although these behaviors in themselves do not indicate autism, an individual with autism is more likely to display them. Many adults with autism learn to understand their own strengths and weaknesses and, with appropriate support, can improve their social skills and manage other challenges, allowing them to integrate successfully into the workplace.

Table 2.1: Common interpretation of behavior of individuals with autism

Observed Behavior	Common Interpretation
Doesn't want to engage in group activities	Socially "out of the loop"
Can't tell that you are annoyed with them	Oblivious to social cues
Talks a lot about a specific topic	Limited/odd interests
Problem maintaining eye contact, or awkwardly changes the subject of conversation	Appears uninterested
Refers to themselves, or their needs, more than seems normal	Appears self-centered
Upset by minor schedule changes	Easily flustered/too sensitive/inflexible
Looks out the window a lot, or jerks his head in the direction of any sudden noises	Easily distracted/daydreaming
Points out others' mistakes	Seems rude/impolite/pedantic

It is important to remember that not all individuals with autism will display all of these behaviors. Each individual on the spectrum is different, and their challenges related to autism will be unique to them.

While the behaviors of individuals with autism may seem inappropriate or odd to you, they may not view themselves in the same way. Few people with autism notice themselves avoiding eye contact or abruptly switching the topic of conversation. When asked, they can often give a logical explanation for their behavior or response to a situation, based on how they processed their thoughts, emotions, and experiences at the time. The overall effect for the individual is somewhat akin to the immigrant experience, where the new immigrant may have ways of doing things that differ from the ways of the vast majority in their recently adopted homeland.

Similarly, most professionals with autism know that in order to succeed, they benefit from using strategies that enable them to accommodate the larger world and the workplace.

Why should your company hire professionals with autism?

In today's economy, it is part of everyone's job to think about how their company performs from a financial perspective. Performance reviews for even the most junior employees will generally have some targets that in some way tie back to company performance. Managers care about turnover and productivity, even if just in their unit. Employees take pride in their company being positioned best among their competitors, and everyone benefits from a work environment that embraces diversity and inclusion.

There is a very compelling reason why companies should be interested in understanding autism and successfully employing individuals on the spectrum: *It's good for business!*

Specifically, the business reasons for employing individuals with autism include:

- reduced staff turnover

- increased productivity

- consumer appeal to a large affinity group

- competitive advantage

- regulatory compliance

- minimal cost for hiring and accommodations.

Reduced staff turnover

The amount of money actually spent to replace a worker will differ from company to company, but the Society for Human Resource Management (SHRM) estimates that "direct replacement costs can reach as high as 50%–60% of an employee's annual salary, with total costs associated with turnover ranging from 90% to 200% of annual salary."[7] A study conducted in 2010 by the Kessler Foundation/National Organization on Disability found that 33% of the employers believed that employees with disabilities were less likely than employees without disabilities to actively search for, and find, another job.[8] Individuals with autism tend to dislike change and will stay in the same job for a long time if the work and the work environment are appropriate.

Increased productivity

Individuals with autism are known for their focus, attention to detail, accuracy, memory of facts and figures, and ability to concentrate on repetitive tasks and procedures. They are often more interested in completing the task at hand than they are in socializing in the office with co-workers. As a result, they are often highly productive employees, particularly of jobs and tasks that others find boring or repetitive.

Consumer appeal to a large affinity group

People affected by autism are one of the largest affinity groups in this country. Add to the 1 in 68 children currently being diagnosed with autism, their parents, grandparents, siblings, aunts and uncles, and first cousins, and you have a population that is over 55 million people, or approximately 17% of the U.S. population. This is a consumer base that is issue-sensitive and, given the choice, will spend their consumer dollars with companies that are known to support individuals on the spectrum. According to the 2013 Cone Communications Social Impact Study:[9]

- 93% of consumers have a more positive image of a company when that company supports a cause.

- 89% of consumers are likely to switch brands to one that is associated with a good cause, given similar price and quality.

- 54% of Americans bought a product associated with a cause over the last 12 months, increasing 170% since 1993.

Here in New York City, for instance, you will sometimes see two or three competing pharmacies within one block of each other. A person touched by autism who knows about the Walgreen's distribution centers that employ 800 people with developmental disabilities is bound to choose Walgreen's over the other stores.

Competitive advantage

A growing number of companies have taken the lead in employing individuals on the autism spectrum. News stories appear almost daily about the efforts of companies such as SAP, Walgreen's, AMC Loews, and Best Buy—to name a few—in employing individuals on the spectrum. Given the size and purchasing power of the autism community, any company that allows its competitors to surpass it in the effort to integrate individuals with autism into their workforce is choosing to cede market share to those who are employing this population.

Regulatory compliance

In September 2013, the U.S. Office of Federal Contract Compliance issued a Final Rule to Section 503 of the Rehabilitation Act saying that all federal contractors and subcontractors should have 7% of their workforce be people with disabilities.[10] A company is considered a federal contractor, or subcontractor, if they have a contract for $10,000 or more with the federal government or an agency of the federal government. This covers most large employers. The rule requires employers to take affirmative steps to hire, retain, and promote qualified individuals with disabilities.

In addition, employers with both federal contracts or subcontracts of $50,000 or more and 50 or more employees must:

- prepare, implement, and maintain a written affirmative action program (AAP) for each of its establishments
- review and update the AAP annually
- make it available for inspection by any employee or applicant for employment, as well as by the Office of Federal Contract Compliance Programs.

To the extent that you can create a more inclusive environment in your company, employees on the spectrum may be encouraged to disclose their disability, helping your employer meet compliance goals for employing individuals with disabilities.

Minimal cost for accommodations and hiring

Employees with Asperger Syndrome do not need costly accommodations. Typical accommodations include clear communication, providing social cues, giving notice of schedule changes, providing short breaks and flexible work hours, replacing fluorescent light bulbs with incandescent lights, and developing an understanding of the behaviors you might see in the workplace.

The perception that hiring a person with a disability costs more than hiring someone without a disability is simply a myth. The Kessler/Cornell study, previously mentioned, found that 62% of the employers found no difference in cost when comparing the hiring of new employees with disabilities with the hiring of new employees without disabilities.

Why should you learn about autism?

Considering the current incidence rates of autism spectrum diagnoses, if you work in a large company, you already work with and manage individuals on the spectrum. These employees will often be found in jobs that are technical in nature, where they perform well on their assigned tasks, but don't fit in with their team or the company culture. More often than not, individuals on the spectrum will be terminated from their job for reasons related to fit, rather than job performance. By recognizing behaviors in the workplace that could be related to an autism spectrum disorder, and utilizing the management techniques and strategies discussed in this book, you could maximize the potential of an employee on the spectrum, and possibly avoid a costly and disruptive termination.

Bullying and professionals with autism

Bullying is an issue in the national forefront today; with the advent of the internet and social media, anonymous bullying has flourished. In 2012, the National Autistic Society of the UK published a study reporting that one third of adults with autism have been bullied or discriminated against at work.[11] People with autism spectrum disorders are often victims of bullying in the workplace due to their inability to "fit in" and their apparent lack of understanding of the many forms of bullying that can occur. Bullying in the social environment may include:

- making rude remarks
- making jokes at the expense of the individual on the spectrum
- acting in a condescending or insulting manner
- humiliating the individual in front of others
- excluding the individual from team or social events
- spreading rumors.

Specifically in the work environment, bullying may also include:

- supervising in an overbearing manner
- denying training or promotion
- constantly criticizing performance

- setting tasks or deadlines that cannot be met
- assigning insufficient work or menial tasks
- taking credit for others' work
- threatening job security, even though performing well.

It is no wonder that individuals on the autism spectrum are particularly susceptible to bullying. They oftentimes lack the ability to understand an organization's chain of command and social landscape. As a result, they will engage in behaviors that can be perceived by their peers as being odd, weird, awkward, inappropriate, annoying, obstinate, aloof, or gullible. They do not understand that one's skills and ability to do the job are not the only factors on which they will be judged, and can be surprised or upset when this is the case. When an individual on the spectrum is bullied at work, it is often exacerbated by the fact that the individual has no support group within the organization to defend him or provide a place of refuge.

"People with Asperger's typically are victims of bullying. If somebody's smiling and they say something to me, I assume they're joking and they're being friendly, not being facetious. When I realize that they were being facetious, it's often too late. And because of that, people that are bullies in the workplace can take advantage of people with Asperger Syndrome."

If you manage an employee who has disclosed that he is on the spectrum, reach out and encourage him to report any bullying to you. If you have an employee who does not fit in with the rest of the team, but who has not disclosed an autism diagnosis, be aware of your team's dynamics and watch for signs of bullying. It should go without saying, always have a zero-tolerance policy for bullying in your workplace, with safe avenues for employees to report bullying.

If you are reading this book, it is likely you have an employee or co-worker who has disclosed they have an autism spectrum disorder or you suspect they might. One of the biggest challenges for both employers and employees with autism is disclosure. Most popular advice on the topic encourages individuals on the spectrum to disclose only if necessary (e.g. they believe they are at risk of being fired for behaviors related to their autism). The next chapter will discuss the issues around disclosure, including the pros and cons of encouraging disclosure among employees you suspect may be on the spectrum but have not disclosed.

Chapter 3

DISCLOSURE AND TYPES OF EMPLOYEES ON THE SPECTRUM

The growing incidence rates of autism (1 in 68 children in the U.S. as of 2014) combined with the fact that 35% of individuals on the spectrum are advancing to college is creating a largely untapped workforce with strong skill sets. Therefore, it is no wonder that *neuro-diversity* in the workplace is a growing topic among employers today. A number of companies, such as SAP, CAI, Microsoft, EY, and Freddie Mac, have been in the news for creating programs focused on hiring individuals with autism spectrum disorders in order to benefit from the unique skill sets they can bring to the workplace. Megan Pierouchakos, a senior diversity specialist at Freddie Mac, considers individuals with autism "an untapped reservoir of talent that we have discovered." She warns that employers who ignore autistic candidates are "overlooking someone who is highly analytical, very focused, and very task-oriented."[12] José Velasco, head of the Autism at Work program at SAP, believes the effects of a neuro-diverse workforce are far-reaching:

> The Autism at Work program has been incredible… It is changing us as a company, how we are looking at our customers and the communities we serve. We have a vision here that the more diverse the company becomes, the better, because that allows us to incorporate more perspectives into our products

and our solutions. If you can tap into perspectives that haven't been brought into the light before, then you can open up a whole new, richer, deeper and broader view of the world.[13]

Pursuing a conscious and coordinated effort to hire individuals with autism allows a company to prepare itself to be an effective employer of neuro-diverse thinkers. Education and training on how to manage professionals with autism, modified recruiting and interviewing practices, clearly defined job roles and responsibilities, and mentoring programs can all allow job candidates on the spectrum to demonstrate their skills and competencies and provide managers with the skill sets needed to support them.

Despite these efforts we read about in the business news, however, employers still officially count very few individuals on the autism spectrum among their employees with disabilities, particularly in their professional ranks. Does this mean that aside from the employers implementing targeted programs to hire individuals on the autism spectrum, most companies do not employ anyone on the spectrum? The answer to this question is a resounding "No!"

Who are these unaccounted-for employees on the autism spectrum in the workforce? The answer lies in the incidence rate of autism diagnoses in children, which has more than doubled over the past 20 years, from 1 in 166 in 2000 to 1 in 68 today. Among the many possible reasons for this increase are more effective diagnostic tools being used by clinicians (psychologists, social workers, and psychiatrists) to evaluate and identify individuals on the spectrum. As a result, it is not uncommon today to hear the story of an adult who was diagnosed as being on the autism spectrum shortly after taking his or her child in for an evaluation for autism. Michael Burry, MD, the hedge fund investor at the center of Michael Lewis's *The Big Short*, is one of those parents. As recounted by Lewis, Burry's wife "handed him the stack of books she had accumulated on autism and related disorders... After a few pages, Michael Burry realized that he was no longer reading about his son but about himself."[14]

Over the past 15 years a growing number of individuals have come forward disclosing that they were diagnosed as being on the autism spectrum as adults, including actress Darryl Hannah; actor Dan Ackroyd; Nobel laureate in Economics Vernon Smith; creator of the comedy series *Community*, Dan Harmon; and Alexis Wineman, Miss Montana and the first Miss America contestant with autism. In working with a global accounting and advisory services firm, we encountered a partner who was diagnosed with Asperger Syndrome around the time his son was diagnosed, yet he had never disclosed at work. After seeing his firm being proactive in hiring and accommodating professionals on the autism spectrum, he became involved in those efforts and eventually disclosed his own diagnosis.

Rising autism incidence rates, coupled with increased diagnosis for adults, are resulting in a trend we are seeing with employers, particularly those with large-scale (5000+ employees) workforces: many of these employers believe they already have employees on the spectrum, but know their numbers are not reflected in the company's diversity data. Whether it is a desire to create an inclusive workplace environment, meet regulatory compliance requirements, or understand how to accommodate employees who have neuro-diverse profiles, these same employers are anxious to promote disclosure in their organizations.

Why disclosure is good for companies

Many reasons exist for wanting employees with autism (or any disability for that matter) to disclose. As discussed in Chapter 2, disclosure is good for business, on multiple levels. Some other reasons are:

- *Employer of choice*—You cannot accommodate what you do not know! If an employee is struggling due to challenges related to autism, you may not be able to help that employee be successful without understanding the root cause of their struggles. If you are an employer that encourages disclosure and provides a supportive workplace for individuals with disabilities, you will become known as an employer of choice within the disability community.

- *Employee engagement*—Not only are individuals on the spectrum your employees, so are many more individuals with a personal connection to autism. Demonstrating your organization is an *autism-friendly* employer increases the engagement of *all* existing employees, particularly those touched by autism through family and friends.

- *Risk management*—Employers are experiencing an increase in the number of all employees with hidden disabilities. Understanding the challenges related to disability will be key in mitigating risks related to litigation.

But possibly most important, disclosure may be necessary to allow an employee to contribute to their maximum potential. As an employer, you want to create an environment that allows all of your employees to do their best for you.

So, how does an employer determine if they have employees on the spectrum, and how do they encourage them to disclose?

The three types of individuals on the spectrum

Professionals on the autism spectrum fall into one of three categories:

- diagnosed and disclosed
- diagnosed and undisclosed
- undiagnosed and undisclosed.

Diagnosed and disclosed

"I think if you tell an employer that you have Asperger's, you're obviously looking for something, or you wouldn't have shared it with them."

For an employer, this is the best situation. Many individuals on the spectrum will be able to tell you where they struggle at work and what types of accommodations and strategies will help them perform to the best of their abilities. Once an employee has disclosed, the manager and the employee can have an open dialogue about what challenges related to autism the employee may face in the workplace and what is needed for them to be successful in their job. Below are some initial steps to take when an employee discloses to you:

1. First and foremost—do not jump to conclusions or make assumptions about what the individual's particular challenges related to autism may or may not be. Every individual on the autism spectrum is different and will experience the impact differently in the workplace.

2. Listen to the employee. Learn why they are disclosing to you and discuss if and how they want to disclose to others at their workplace.

3. Check with your human resource compliance team to determine your local laws regarding proof of disability, accommodation requirements, and disclosure to others.

4. If you are unfamiliar with autism and/or Asperger Syndrome, learn about it (reading this book should help!).

5. Develop a plan for any needed accommodations and additional disclosure to others with your human resources support and the employee.

Diagnosed and undisclosed

"I really thought about telling them, but during the interview I always worry about it's not going to give me a fair shot at getting the job, that they might look different at me."

Many individuals who have been diagnosed with an autism spectrum disorder struggle with the question of whether or not to disclose, particularly to a potential or current employer. The decision to disclose is a personal one and driven by many factors. In 2011, the American Association of People with Disabilities did a study[15] to find out why employees with hidden disabilities do not disclose. The top five reasons were:

1. Risk of being fired/not hired

2. Concern that employer may focus on disability

3. Risk of losing health care

4. Fear of limited opportunities

5. Concern that supervisor may not be supportive

While many employers assume people don't disclose due to a desire for privacy, that is not the case. Privacy was number nine on the list of reasons for not disclosing, with less than one third of individuals polled citing that as a concern.

We believe it is usually in the best long-term interest of the individual and the employer if an individual discloses. However, we do advise individuals who have been diagnosed with autism that there is no right or wrong answer to the question of disclosure. We encourage them to talk to those they know well and who understand the dynamics of the employment world, but stress the importance of being comfortable with whatever decision they make.

Undiagnosed and undisclosed

Obviously, this is the most difficult situation for both an employee and an employer to deal with in a work environment.

Both parties may be trying to manage through the challenges that are associated with autism without understanding the underlying causes of certain behaviors and the best strategies for handling them.

Although we strongly discourage any employer from "diagnosing" an employee he suspects is on the spectrum (or with any type of disability), he can encourage sensitivity and understanding of neuro-diverse individuals in general. An astute manager can learn how to observe the behaviors of his employees, compare them to the behaviors described in this book and utilize the management strategies discussed to allow his employees to function at their best.

How do I encourage someone to disclose?

Most individuals will disclose a disability to their employer for one of two reasons—they trust that their employer will understand their situation and provide reasonable accommodations to the extent necessary, or they need accommodations and are at risk of losing their job without them. When thinking about disclosure, the ideal situation is to have employees with disabilities disclose when things are going well, regardless of the need for an accommodation, rather than as a protective measure when they fear being terminated.

So, how do you encourage employees on the spectrum to disclose? Creating an *autism-friendly environment* is the most effective way to encourage disclosure. Below are ways in which a company can strive to be autism-friendly.

- *Training*—Train human resource staff, managers, and colleagues about autism spectrum disorders, the unique skill sets of individuals on the spectrum, and some of the behavioral differences they may exhibit in the workplace. This can reassure employees on the spectrum that their differing behaviors and needed accommodations will not be misunderstood as a liability by co-workers and supervisors.

- *Inclusion*—Promote efforts to hire diverse individuals, including those with neuro-diverse profiles.

- *Employee Resource Groups (ERGs)*—Use ERGs for employees with disabilities to participate in driving your disability diversity programs and practices.

- *Avenues for disclosure*—Create multiple channels within your company for individuals to disclose (e.g. employee assistance programs, human resources, direct manager, intranet portal, etc.).

- *Mentoring programs*—Develop mentoring programs for neuro-diverse employees that pair experienced employees with neuro-diverse profiles with the newer employees who identify as neuro-diverse. Assign a neuro-typical mentor to neuro-diverse employees to help guide them through the social and cultural norms of your organization.

Disclosure does not have to be an all-or-nothing decision for an employee either. Partial disclosure to a carefully selected group of individuals within your organization (e.g. a human resource representative, a direct manager, and a few select colleagues) may provide the support to an individual on the spectrum that they need while allowing him maintain some degree of privacy.

If you are reading this book, it is likely you know or believe you have at least one employee on the autism spectrum, and are looking for answers on how to provide an environment that will allow that individual to perform to the best of his abilities. You may be a small business, employing only a handful of people, or you may be a multinational organization with tens of thousands of employees around the world. Regardless of your size, the task of providing effective accommodations to someone with a hidden disability that you might not completely understand may seem daunting.

Implementing the types of programs listed above may be out of reach for your organization or take more time than you have to address the immediate needs of an employee on the spectrum. This book is designed to give you practical advice that you can implement immediately, in workplaces of any size. We have grouped the challenges professionals on the autism spectrum may face at work into three areas:

- social issues

- work performance

- sensory issues.

Understanding the effect of autism in these areas is an important step toward creating an autism-friendly work environment that will benefit *all* employees. We encourage all employers to understand and embrace programs to create an inclusive workplace environment, allowing employees with hidden disabilities to disclose freely. At the same time, we hope you will find this book useful in implementing successful techniques and management strategies to work with your colleagues on the autism spectrum on a daily basis.

Part Two

SOCIAL ISSUES AT WORK

Chapter 4

INTRODUCTION TO SOCIAL ISSUES AT WORK

The failure to "fit in" at work is one of the most common challenges for people with autism. The workplace is a social environment that requires interaction and cooperation among employees. Lunches, team meetings, the holiday party, and even hallway or water cooler conversations are all opportunities for colleagues to work together or just chat. Although autism is considered a "hidden disability," the observable behavior of colleagues with autism is often described as annoying, odd, rude, and uncaring. While many people on the spectrum may want to socialize with others, their social-skill deficits can make these interactions awkward. As a result, some individuals with autism avoid socializing as much as they can and are often considered "loners."

All offices have unwritten social rules that can be difficult for a person with autism to decipher. For example, in some companies, employees chip in to buy birthday cake and a gift for co-workers. In other offices, team members will eat lunch together, plan a weekend day outing once or twice a year or arrange a team community service day. Someone with autism may find these activities uninteresting or unimportant and decline to participate, potentially alienating his team members. Alternatively, an employee on the spectrum may join the lunch group, but talk in detail about a topic without asking others about *their* interests.

Some individuals with autism may also interpret office policies in a very literal fashion, assuming that an "open door policy" means that all office doors must be kept open at all times, or that anyone can enter a manager's or colleague's office at any time. And, although people with autism tend to be honest, they may not realize that pointing out a co-worker's recent weight gain can be insensitive and rude.

The "hidden curriculum" of the workplace

The *hidden curriculum* is social information that everyone knows without being taught, and it is the basis for many of the social rules in the workplace assumed to be understood by all. It involves the deciphering of nonverbal cues such as body language, slang expressions, and other subtle social cues, as well as comprehending the meaning of a gesture, facial expression, or tone of voice that does not match what someone says. Understanding the hidden curriculum in the workplace is essential, because it comprises what most people consider to be "polite" behavior and helps employees interpret the demands and expectations of the people with whom they work.

The hidden curriculum can be especially confusing to individuals with autism. If you have found yourself thinking any of these when interacting with a colleague, then most likely you are dealing with a hidden curriculum issue:[16]

- "I shouldn't have to tell you, but…"

- "I assumed that…"

- "I expected that…"

- "It's obvious that…"

- "Everyone knows that…"

Theory of mind

The hidden curriculum is based largely on our ability to understand what other people are thinking and to behave appropriately. At first, a child knows only what is in his own mind, but he gradually learns how his behavior affects others from their reactions to it. As you move from childhood to adulthood, you acquire a great deal of unconscious knowledge about how the behavior of others reflects their inner thoughts and feelings. By noticing the reactions to your own behavior, you gain an understanding of how others perceive you. Although it is impossible to know definitively what is in another person's mind, we *imagine* what they might be thinking or anticipate their reactions based on what they say, as well as on the nonverbal cues in their face, posture, and tone of voice. Researchers call this capacity to understand the perspective of others *theory of mind*, but most people think of it as "being in someone else's shoes."

Effective communication and ease in social interactions depend on theory of mind. Individuals on the spectrum typically struggle in this area and often miss or misinterpret reactions to their behavior. They may talk nonstop, interrupt, or have difficulty seeing past their own agenda and point of view. Consequently, people with autism may appear insensitive or rude, because they often fail to anticipate the impact of their comments and behaviors or consider the opinions, plans, and points of view of others.

The role of context

Theory of mind involves more than what we observe in another person; we spontaneously integrate additional information such as our surroundings and our own related experiences and feelings. However, the meaning of any social behavior is rarely absolute or fixed. For example, when you see a friend crying, how do you respond? Most likely your answer is, "It depends on the situation," because tears can be due to various emotions: sadness, joy, anger, or a physical reaction from cutting onions.

In the blink of an eye you instinctively assemble input from many different sources of information into the "big picture" of why your friend is crying and respond appropriately.

Another word for "the situation" is *context*, and being aware or sensitive to context is an important component of theory of mind, as well as how we process information in general. Context allows us to focus on what is important and ignore what is not. It helps us find the right meaning when information is vague or incomplete, or when multiple meanings are possible. Most importantly, context allows us to filter multiple sources of information and combine the most relevant into a coherent whole.

Individuals on the spectrum have difficulty with context, and tend to respond to one piece of information at a time. This presents challenges in social situations, because the context is constantly changing and their interpretation may be limited or inaccurate:

> *"For instance, I'd walk into a room, and somebody's crying. Well, I don't know why that person's crying—I know I'm in the room, and that person's upset. So I must have upset that person. Because I have no way of putting myself in the situation or thinking, 'OK, something happened before I was in the room, so therefore that person's crying because of something else, and not necessarily something I did.'"*

According to Dr. Peter Vermeulen, an expert in the field of autism, people on the spectrum are "context blind": they may be aware of the context but not able to apply or use it spontaneously,[17] resulting in behavior that is inflexible and often inappropriate. However, Dr. Vermeulen feels that individuals with autism *can* learn to use context if we "push the context button" to help them find the "right" meaning of social situations so they can behave appropriately.[18]

Dealing with an employee's annoying, inappropriate, or disruptive social behavior involves looking at it from *the individual's perspective*, as well as that of the colleague or manager affected by it. By taking the *specifics of the situation* (i.e. the context) into account, we can use our own "theory of mind" to understand how people on the spectrum view the world. Through this approach, we can help them identify *when* and *why* behavior is not appropriate and offer alternative ways to act in various situations.

Typical social challenges at work

Every job has social aspects related to theory of mind and the hidden curriculum, from informal socializing with colleagues to understanding the nuances of office politics. Individuals with autism may experience challenges with:

- talking too much or giving too much information
- saying inappropriate things
- interrupting or being repetitive
- making or maintaining eye contact
- reading facial expressions and recognizing faces
- interpreting sarcasm or idioms
- dealing with social situations and office politics.

Disclosure and accommodations for social challenges

When an employee has difficulty with social interactions in his workplace, a manager will need to try different strategies until one is found that works. As with any disability, *disclosure* allows a manager and colleagues to respectfully engage in an *open dialogue* with the disclosed person about how his behavior affects others in social situations and how to most effectively address it.

Many individuals with an autism spectrum diagnosis who are disclosed are aware of their social challenges and what accommodations they need to be successful. However, the most effective accommodation for social challenges at work is better *understanding* on the part of managers and colleagues of how people on the spectrum think and experience these social situations, especially if the behavior in question really does not affect job performance or disrupt the work environment. In addition to understanding, *strategies* and *rules* offer specific ways you can "push the context button" to help an employee with autism address various social interactions and learn from them (see Table 4.1).

Table 4.1: Types of accommodations for social issues

	Definition	Example
Understanding	Ways of looking at the behavior within the context of the autism spectrum	People on the spectrum generally feel that "small talk" is not necessary.
Strategies	Simple tactics that you can use	Give a simple cue to stop talking.
Rules	Concrete statements that define parameters of acceptable behavior	"When at work, don't make comments about religion."

In the next two chapters, *Talking* and *Social Interaction*, we will discuss the most common behaviors related to challenges in these areas and the various accommodations to deal with them effectively.

Chapter 5

TALKING

Talking has been an essential part of the human experience ever since the dawn of mankind, when our ancestors told stories around the communal campfire. Through talking we share our dreams, defeats, joys, and sorrows, and, in turn, listen to other people talk about theirs.

Communication involves a give and take between talking and listening, as well as interpreting the reactions of the listener, so we can respond appropriately. Skilled communicators within a company are often admired and promoted, and individuals who have difficulty communicating with colleagues often engender negative responses such as:

- "When I speak to him, it's like talking to a brick wall."

- "All he talks about is himself."

- "He doesn't know what he's talking about."

Generally, talking is a pleasurable experience: we talk to connect with others, communicate information, and share our thoughts and feelings. *Context* and *theory of mind* play an important role in the *hidden curriculum* related to conversing with others; what we say in one situation may not be appropriate in another context. For example, although we value honesty and truthfulness, sometimes we tell "white lies" to spare someone's feelings.

Individuals with autism, however, often find it difficult to engage in appropriate conversation: they talk nonstop about a specific interest, inundate us with unnecessary detail, or bluntly make statements that are generally considered rude. These behaviors can be annoying and frustrating to co-workers.

In this chapter, we will cover the most common problems with respect to talking for individuals with autism: talking too much or repeatedly, speaking inappropriately, and talking at the wrong time.

On a positive note:

- People on the spectrum are eager to share their knowledge and often become subject matter experts and the "go-to" person for that information in their departments.

- Since they do not see the need for "small talk," they tend to concentrate on work without requiring time to socialize.

- When asked for an opinion, they will give an honest answer without regard to office politics.

As you read this chapter, please remember that not all individuals with autism will display all of the behaviors discussed. Each individual on the spectrum is different, and their challenges related to autism will be unique to them.

Section 5.1: Will he EVER stop talking?

Topics covered

- Gives TMI (Too Much Information)
- Dominates the conversation
- Talks in monologues
- Cannot make small talk
- Speaks repetitively, especially about special interests

Are you seeing these behaviors?

- You casually mention to a co-worker that you enjoy a particular TV show, and now whenever he sees you, he recalls facts about the cast and the latest episode in excruciating detail. *And you think to yourself, "Will he EVER stop talking?"*

- When conversing with other employees, a colleague tends to dominate the conversation, or sees little point in pursuing a conversation about topics that are of little interest to him.

What are the underlying issues?

One of the primary ways we connect with each other is through talking, and the two-way conversation we take for granted is a complex activity that involves spontaneously processing the back and forth information of what someone says to us and our response to it. Conversations are not necessarily linear, and topics can switch quickly, especially when several people are talking together at the lunch table or in a meeting. For *neurotypicals* (people *not* on the autism spectrum), conversation with different people in various situations is intuitive; but for individuals with autism, this process is challenging. Consequently, they may have the desire to connect with others, but lack the communication skills to do so.

People with autism are known for talking *at* people rather than *with* them. Keeping track of the thread of a fast-paced conversation while filtering out important information from less significant details is difficult for people on the spectrum. They often have a hard time thinking of what to say, especially when there could be multiple responses to a statement. For example, think of all the ways in which you might respond to a colleague who mentions that he fell from a ladder over the weekend: *Were you hurt? What were you doing on a ladder? How do you feel now?* An individual with autism, however, might focus on the ladder instead of the person and launch into a monologue about which ladders are the safest.

Talking about a fixed topic of interest allows someone on the spectrum to maintain control over social situations that seem to have unlimited parameters. If you casually mention something to a colleague with autism that pertains to his interests, he might track you down the next day and inundate you with a myriad of facts about it.

Talking and theory of mind

Although people on the autism spectrum tend to have very limited interests, they have a tremendous depth of focus in those areas. They often become expert in a narrow, sometimes esoteric, subject area. They are passionate about what they know and proud of their ability to research and retain this knowledge. Sharing what they know with others is their mode of connecting, although it may not seem that way to the person on the receiving end of a monologue!

Individuals on the autism spectrum struggle with *theory of mind*, so they do not understand that someone may not be interested in the same subject or level of detail that they find so fascinating. They tend to miss the meaning of facial expressions and body language that serve as subtle cues to stop talking.

"I'll start speaking about articles in the Wall Street Journal and take them into a depth that most people just kind of gloss over—you know, compare and contrast different economies and markets and things like that—and people just tend to move away from me when I talk that way."

An individual with autism may dominate a conversation because he does not realize how long he has been talking about a favorite topic, or he may try to steer the discussion back to his comfort zone when the conversation shifts or he feels lost and unable to contribute.

Too much information

When someone asks you a question, the context of the situation helps you decide *what* information and *how much* to provide. An employee on the spectrum, however, has difficulty differentiating which details are relevant. He might respond to "Tell me about yourself" by reciting the specifics of the date, time, location, and hospital of his birth, then start to chronicle his life. A request for a project update might result in a litany of every single meeting he had and with whom. One employer described it as, "I would ask for a brief synopsis of the American Revolution, and I'd get the whole encyclopedia version from you."

"Small talk" (i.e. conversation that is light in nature with the purpose of filling time or a gap in conversation) also presents a challenge for an individual on the spectrum, who may feel it makes little sense to discuss the weather for the sake of being friendly. Similarly, a coffee break conversation about the weekend may not seem relevant to an employee with autism, if he is not directly affected by it, or if it doesn't directly relate to work.

> "If they are all talking about football or NASCAR or what they're going to do this weekend, I don't really care, and I'll typically try to stay away from that. If somebody wants to talk about early American history or computers, I'll talk your ear off for hours."

Repetition

Being repetitive is not the sole domain of individuals with autism—we have all encountered colleagues who bring up every aspect of "the big game" for several days, talk repeatedly about a new car, or who show you vacation pictures every day for a week. After all, it is only human to want to share those things that interest us. Eventually these people move on to other topics, but a colleague on the spectrum may not.

For individuals with autism, repeatedly talking about a topic of interest offers a familiarity and sameness that helps them feel more comfortable and in control when interacting with others. Unfortunately, they may have difficulty regulating their behavior or interpreting social cues, so what started as an appropriate response to a casual question, or an attempt at conversation, often takes on a life of its own that extends far beyond the original interaction, leaving colleagues walking in the other direction to avoid hearing about the same topic for the tenth time.

What can you do about an employee who talks too much?

The most effective way to help employees with autism who have issues related to talking is to understand that most likely their intention is to connect socially—something that does not come naturally to people on the spectrum.

Within the context of a social interaction, it may be necessary to coach both the employee with autism and the people who work with him, so that he doesn't become ostracized. Explain to colleagues that it is totally appropriate to respectfully, but directly, interrupt an individual on the autism spectrum and say, "That was very interesting, but I need to get back to my desk now."

It is annoying to hear the same topic repeatedly, and the individual with autism may not pick up on the social cues that signal a person has lost interest. Place limits on the behavior by telling him, "You've already told me a lot about X, let's talk about something else." If an employee who is disclosed does this constantly, you can sit down with him and agree on a nonverbal signal. For example, you can hold up your hand after two or three minutes of talking to let him know that he has talked enough, or that it is time for someone else to talk.

"I have developed a few cues for people to let me know if I do talk too long, or if they just want me to be quiet. I usually just tell people to say 'It's enough' or 'You've been talking for a long time'."

If a colleague wants to be included in social settings (e.g. the lunch table), you can give him coaching and rules about what topics are not appropriate (such as religion) and how to engage in "small talk," even if he is not particularly interested in what is being discussed.

> *"I started to become very interested in reading about sports— sports are a good connection; it's superficial, but it's a good connection."*

When an employee consistently gives "too much information," identify the situations where a short answer is sufficient, such as a casual greeting or coffee break conversations, then rehearse an appropriate response that is limited to less than a minute. If you need a quick update on a project, cue him that you only have a few minutes, so you only want the key points.

Related material

- Chapter 6: Social Interaction

Section 5.2: He said WHAT?

Topics covered

- Says inappropriate things
- Brings up inappropriate topics
- Insults co-workers

Are you seeing these behaviors?

- Your team is gathering in the conference room, chatting with one of the members who just returned from a three-week vacation. Another colleague walks in and comments, "Oh my goodness, Sue, you got fat!" *And you think to yourself, "He said WHAT?"*

- Your co-workers complain that a colleague has been sitting with them at lunch and talking endlessly about the different forms of bacteria that exist on each person's food.

- During a team meeting, in response to the team leader's recommendation, one of your co-workers laughs and says, "That's the stupidest idea I've ever heard!"

What are the underlying issues?

As mentioned in the introduction to Part Two, appropriate or "polite" behavior is largely based on the *hidden curriculum*, that is, the social rules we assimilate about various interpersonal situations as we go through life. As a young child, you learned how to behave within social norms through rules such as "Share your toys" or "Don't talk back to grownups." As you matured, your parents and teachers relied less on black-and-white rules and focused more on *why* certain behaviors were not appropriate or *how* your behavior affected another person. Similarly, many of the hidden curriculum rules are not explicitly taught, but are learned through observing the consequences of breaking or maintaining social rules in various settings.

The hidden curriculum depends on *theory of mind*, which allows us to imagine how someone will think, feel, and react, given the circumstances. We use theory of mind every day when interacting with others to make judgments as to whether a person's behavior is in line with moral or social norms, and then respond accordingly. However, even commonplace interactions are highly unstructured, complex, and far from predictable; and what is considered appropriate in one context may not be in another.

Individuals on the spectrum view the world as highly structured; they tend to think in terms of black and white or right and wrong, which conflicts with the reality that people do not always think or act the same way in every situation. People with autism may appear insensitive or rude, because they often fail to anticipate the impact of their comments and behaviors or consider the opinions, plans, and points of view of others. They may say things that are inappropriate or bring up topics such as religion, race, extreme political views, or highly personal information, without realizing that these are inappropriate in a social situation. A person on the spectrum might make his co-workers uncomfortable during casual conversations by relating *his* special interest in an area that other people may find offensive, shocking, or highly graphic.

In addition to problems with understanding hidden curriculum rules, an individual on the spectrum may inadvertently insult co-workers because he has difficulty *filtering* what he says or expresses his opinion in a harsh fashion, such as "That's a really stupid idea!" or "Everybody knows THAT won't work!"

Context and the hidden curriculum

Knowing if one's behavior is appropriate or not depends largely on *context*, or the surrounding circumstances of a social interaction. The social world, particularly that of the hidden curriculum, is complex and depends on our ability to spontaneously gather the relevant details of a social interaction so we can understand it. No two social situations are *exactly* alike, so we *generalize* from one to another by noting the similarities and applying the relevant social rules. For instance, a child who is reprimanded for talking back to a teacher eventually learns not to speak that way to *any* figure of authority.

Individuals with autism are highly attuned to changes in their environment, including minor differences that might seem insignificant to others (see Part Four: Sensory Issues at Work). Generalization of hidden curriculum rules is more difficult for a person on the spectrum, because he is more likely to notice what is *different* between similar social situations, rather than what they have in common. As a result, an individual on the spectrum may perceive a social situation as being unrelated to similar social situations, making it difficult to know which social rule applies,[19] or realize that he has said something inappropriate. For example, an employee who has been told by his manager that a certain topic is "off limits when talking to people at lunch" may not realize that the same rule applies to the workplace in general. However, individuals with autism *can* learn to interact appropriately with their colleagues when they are given explicit social rules as well as an explanation of the various situations to which a rule might apply.

Truthfulness

"I didn't realize how my behavior or my actions or my words would affect what other people thought or felt. I could easily have gotten into some trouble. Luckily I never got into any major trouble, but I'm sure that I got into minor trouble more times than I could count."

People on the spectrum have difficulty understanding another person's perspective, so they tend to view their way of thinking as the only way. They live in a fact-based world and are notoriously "truthful." If you ask an employee with autism a question, even rhetorically, be prepared for an honest, direct answer! For example, to most people, "Would you mind…?" is generally understood as a polite request, not a question. An individual on the spectrum, however, might interpret the phrase literally and truthfully answer "Yes" if he has something else he would rather do.

The ability to lie is a normal aspect of a child's development. A "white lie" is a part of the hidden curriculum and depends on theory of mind; it involves intentionally placing in another person's mind an idea that is not true, which is difficult for an individual with autism.[20] We sometimes tell a "white lie" to spare someone's feelings or smooth over a situation at work, but an employee with autism may unintentionally insult a co-worker by pointing out what he assumes to be an obvious fact, such as a noticeable weight gain, without considering the consequences of what he said.

What can you do about an employee who says inappropriate or insulting things?

Because of difficulties with understanding the hidden curriculum, providing *explicit rules* for appropriate social behavior at your workplace is very important when dealing with an employee on the spectrum. Directly communicating the specific guidelines for how people in your organization are expected to behave leaves little room for interpretation and reduces the anxiety that many people on the spectrum feel about not knowing the proper things to say and do.

For example, in some organizations talking about politics is very open and accepted, and the heated arguments that ensue are therefore completely appropriate for that workplace; in other organizations this is definitely not the case. An effective strategy is to create a "Do Not Talk About" list that includes sensitive topics—such as politics, religion, sexual orientation, and ethnicity—as well as special interests of the individual that might make other co-workers uncomfortable. The list could also include comments that the employee might make about a co-worker's appearance that, while accurate, might prove embarrassing, insulting, or hurtful, such as one's weight, breasts, or any physical abnormalities, if the employee has a tendency to make such observations out loud.

Address a social indiscretion by calmly explaining how it affected the other person, and if appropriate, practice a simple apology. Clearly stating a social rule, as well as the relevant scenarios for which the same rule might apply, will help the employee know how to behave in similar situations in the future.[21]

Sometimes the issue is not *what* is being said, but *who* is being addressed (e.g. the co-worker who cites every problematic aspect of a project to a Managing Director or CEO). An employee on the spectrum may need rules about:

- who he may contact (either verbally or via email)
- how they should be addressed
- what level of detail or feedback is appropriate.

Explain to the employee that when a colleague or supervisor says, "Would you mind...?" they are not asking a yes/no question but are making a request.

If an employee on the spectrum criticizes a co-worker or makes work-related comments others find insulting, you can sit down with the employee and teach him ways to "reframe" his observations by asking a question. For example, a statement such as "That's a stupid idea!" or "Everybody knows you should be using XYZ" might be reframed as *"Have you thought about using XYZ?"* or *"How would you deal with XYZ?"* This not only reduces the harsh tone of a blunt response, but allows the individual to make his point as well as get more information from the other person.

Keep in mind that many people on the spectrum do want to engage with others, and it is generally not their intention to be insulting, critical, or inappropriate. Coaching an employee with autism on appropriate topics of conversation and responses in your workplace is generally very effective. However, if an individual persists in making the same mistakes, a manager can help the individual maintain a list of "safe" topics and ask him to practice.

Related material

- Chapter 6: Social Interaction

Section 5.3: Not now!

Topics covered

- Talks at the wrong time
- Interrupts
- Repeats explanations from the beginning when interrupted
- Cannot drop a topic or opinion

Are you seeing these behaviors?

- The CEO is giving a presentation on the quarterly results and informally says, "If anyone has any questions, feel free to interrupt me." A member of your staff proceeds to call out questions every few minutes without raising his hand. *And you think to yourself, "Not now!"*

- One of your employees disagrees with his team's decision on the direction of a project and will not drop it. Whenever a team meeting focuses on the project's forward progress, he describes in detail how the project is going in the wrong direction.

- You have asked a colleague to update you on a project. When you interrupt him to ask a question, he answers, then proceeds to start his update from the beginning.

What are the underlying issues?

For individuals on the spectrum, talking at the "wrong time" often involves not understanding the *context* or "big picture" of the interaction, including the type of audience as well as the situation. Most people refer to this as "reading the room", and understand the *hidden curriculum* rules against barging into a manager's office or the nonverbal cues that signal that this is not a good time to discuss something. Understanding the perspective of another person (*theory of mind*) plays a large part, as an employee with autism may assume that a colleague's or manager's agenda matches his own. He may also fail to realize that how he expresses his opinions and ideas in one setting may not apply to another. For example, in an informal brainstorming session, people might be encouraged to call out ideas as they think of them, while during a team meeting, they are generally expected to wait until recognized before speaking or not speak at all during a formal presentation.

Interrupting and being interrupted

Similarly, an employee may not understand that a presentation to a group needs to move forward without interruption, and that "feel free to interrupt me" is not always to be taken literally. People on the autism spectrum are often literal, sequential thinkers. For example, when someone explains something that they do not understand, they will most likely interrupt with a question, as they cannot tuck it away in a corner of their brain while they listen. When their sequencing of thought stops, they can lose track of what a person is saying and will often address what is in their mind at that moment.

Although people on the spectrum have an amazing capacity to remember facts and detailed information, they may have difficulty keeping several things in mind at the same time, referred to as *working memory*. They need to go through an explanation from point to point in a logical and linear manner, or they can lose focus. Most of us have an internal "pause" button that allows us to mark a spot when interrupted, and then pick up where we left off. However, if you interrupt an individual with autism as he explains something, he might need to start the explanation from the beginning when he resumes.

Repeatedly asking questions or voicing concerns

Sometimes an employee on the spectrum will repeatedly ask multiple questions about the same topic. When faced with a new project or task, most of us first try to understand the "big picture," then fill in the details as we go. This flexibility in thinking allows us to tolerate a certain amount of vagueness, so we can move forward while we get more information. People on the autism spectrum have a low tolerance for vagueness or uncertainty because they live in a rules-based world, where every piece of the puzzle is part of the whole and therefore essential. For example, when an employee on the spectrum is told to work around a low-priority aspect of a project, he may persist in questioning the reasons why he has been asked to do it.

We all occasionally ruminate about something that is the cause of worry or anxiety, as when you cannot sleep because of an upcoming tax audit or medical procedure. Individuals with autism are constantly dealing with anxiety, particularly at work, where just getting through the day generates worry about whether they are meeting the expectations. Consequently, they might repeatedly ask a colleague the same question or express their concern or opinion over a work matter, even though the other person has already answered the question, acknowledged the concern, or resolved it.

When an employee on the spectrum is anxious and expresses the same concern or asks the same question over and over again, a natural reaction is to tell him to "drop it," "stop worrying about it," or "relax." However, research shows that when you instruct someone to suppress or hide their emotions, they tend to exhibit the emotions more strongly![22]

What can you do about an employee who talks at the wrong time?

Explicit rules are the best way to deal with talking at the wrong time and interrupting. Provide rules to an employee on the spectrum regarding when it is appropriate to interrupt and when it is not, and stress that merely saying "excuse me" does not give the individual license to interrupt.

If you have an employee on the spectrum that tends to interrupt you, it may be that he is not understanding something or having difficulty following you, so deliver information in smaller bits, periodically stopping to allow time for clarification or questions. In general, based on the type of discussion you are having, you can give a rule as to when would be the appropriate time to break in; for example, "Let me cover this level of information which I believe might answer your question, and if it does not, I'll give you a chance to ask questions."

To help an individual with autism get through his own explanation or presentations, try not to interrupt him until he has finished. If his train of thought does get interrupted, try to summarize the main points he has made so far, and suggest he resume from that point.

Generally, neuro-typicals deal with repetitive thoughts by actively shifting their thinking to something else—this is very difficult for an individual with autism to do on his own. You can, however, help him shift from a negative scenario by suggesting he focus on something more constructive, such as a possible solution or improvement.

Understand that some repetitive behaviors are related to trying to connect socially or to trying to do one's job well. You can acknowledge an employee's concern while placing limits on his behavior by saying, "I hear you. Let's put that aside for the moment and come back to it later."

When an employee repeatedly voices concerns about a work-related topic such as the direction of a project, the reliability of a calculation or the suitability of a procedure, you can try to redirect his ruminating behavior in a more constructive way by saying, "Summarize your top concerns on one page so I can refer to it." If the issue has already been resolved, acknowledge his concern, then elicit his help moving forward; for example, "I know you are concerned about X—how can we deal with this issue now that we're moving in another direction?"

Related material

- Chapter 9: Time Management
- Chapter 10: Work Quality

Talking: Accommodations summary

The *hidden curriculum* is social information that everyone knows without being taught, and it is the basis for many of the social rules in the workplace that are assumed to be understood by all. Understanding the hidden curriculum is based largely on our ability to perceive what other people are thinking and then behave appropriately. Researchers call this capacity to understand the perspective of others *theory of mind*, but most people think of it as "being in someone else's shoes."

Individuals on the spectrum typically struggle with the hidden curriculum and often miss or misinterpret reactions to their behavior. They may talk nonstop, interrupt, or have difficulty seeing past their own agenda and perspective. Consequently, people with autism may appear insensitive or rude, because they often fail to anticipate the impact of their comments and behaviors or consider the opinions, plans, and points of view of others.

Social behavior is rarely absolute or fixed, so we depend on *context* to understand the nuances of each situation. Awareness and sensitivity to context is an important component of theory of mind, which involves more than what we observe in another person; we spontaneously integrate additional information such as our surroundings and our own related experiences and feelings. However, individuals on the spectrum may not be able to simultaneously process more than one piece of information, so they may not accurately determine the context of social interactions or may miss it entirely.

Context and *theory of mind* play an important role in the *hidden curriculum* relative to conversing with others; what we say in one situation may not be appropriate in another context. For example, although we value honesty and truthfulness, sometimes we tell "white lies" to spare someone's feelings. Individuals with autism can find it difficult to engage in appropriate conversation—they may talk nonstop about a specific interest, bluntly make statements that are generally considered rude, or inundate us with unnecessary detail. As a result, a manager may need to work with the employee on the skills related to:

- talking too much

- saying inappropriate things

- interrupting or fixating on a topic.

> Keep in mind that many people on the spectrum do want to engage with others, and it is generally not their intention to be insulting, critical, or inappropriate.

Coaching an employee with autism and the people who work with him on how to put limits on the length of conversations is an effective way to assist individuals who may talk too much.

- Explain to colleagues that it is totally appropriate to directly but respectfully interrupt an individual on the autism spectrum and say, "That was very interesting, but I need to get back to my desk now."

- Develop a nonverbal cue (e.g. a hand signal) for an employee who is disclosed to inform him that it is time to conclude a conversation or give someone else a turn to talk.

- Place limits on repetitive topics of conversation by telling the employee, "You've already told me a lot about X, let's talk about something else."

- Practice delivering short answers with the employee for recurring situations (e.g. weekly staff meeting updates, casual conversations in the break room, etc.).

Providing guidance and/or rules about what topics are not appropriate (such as religion) and how to engage in "small talk," in social settings, such as the lunch table, will help avoid uncomfortable situations for everyone.

- Create a "Do Not Talk About" list that includes sensitive topics—such as politics, religion, sexual orientation, personal appearance of co-workers, and ethnicity—as well as special interests of the individual that might make other co-workers uncomfortable.

- Address social indiscretions by calmly explaining how it affected the other person, and if appropriate, practice a simple apology.

Extending these rules to work situations will allow employees on the spectrum to avoid offending colleagues or committing workplace faux pas.

- Provide guidelines on who the employee should contact (either verbally or via email), how they should be addressed, and what level of detail or feedback is appropriate on work-related matters.

- Explain to the employee that when a colleague or supervisor says, "Would you mind...?" they are not asking a yes/no question but are making a request.

- Teach the employee ways to "reframe" his observations that others may find critical or insulting. For example, a statement such as "That's a stupid idea!" or "Everybody knows you should be using XYZ" might be reframed as "*Have you thought about using XYZ?*" or "*How would you deal with XYZ?*"

An employee with autism may interrupt or talk out of turn, making it difficult to move along a meeting or conversation. In this situation you can:

- Provide rules regarding when it is appropriate to interrupt and when it is not, and stress that merely saying "excuse me" does not give the individual license to interrupt.

- Deliver information in smaller bits. If an employee continues to interrupt, periodically stop to allow time for clarification or questions, in case he is not understanding something or having difficulty following you.

- Try not to interrupt an employee when he gives an explanation or presentation. If his train of thought does get interrupted, try to summarize the main points he has made so far, and suggest he resume from that point.

Some individuals may fixate on their view of how a project should be completed, slowing the progress of the team.

- Help employees shift from a contrary position by suggesting they focus on something more constructive, such as a possible solution or improvement.

- Place limits on an employee's behavior when he repeatedly expresses the same concern by saying, "I hear you. Let's put that aside for the moment and come back to it later."

Chapter 6

SOCIAL INTERACTION

In a typical workplace, employees need to work together to solve problems, meet deadlines and maximize productivity. Coffee breaks, cafeterias, and company gatherings are all part of the social landscape of many businesses. Tactfulness, flexibility, and being a team player are all qualities that we appreciate in others; however, these qualities are challenging for employees on the spectrum. In their absence, the impressions of co-workers might be:

- "He is so rude."

- "He just doesn't fit in."

- "He always needs to be right."

The ability to interact and communicate effectively, pleasantly, and appropriately in social environments is generally referred to as *soft skills*, *people skills*, or *social intelligence*, and in the workplace they can be the deciding factor in whether someone is hired and how far someone advances.

Social intelligence requires that you not only imagine *what* another person may be thinking and feeling, but also determine *why* he might have those thoughts and emotions. We get information from a person's facial expressions, body language, and tone of voice as well as the actual words spoken, and then evaluate how it relates to the current situation as well as similar situations in the past and respond accordingly.

Much of this process is spontaneous. We are not consciously aware of how we interpret social cues, understand people's motivations, and respond appropriately, so it is difficult to imagine what life is like for those who do not possess these skills. Our own theory of mind may help us understand, at least to some degree, what it is like to lose one's sight or hearing. However, it is much more difficult to "stand in the shoes" of someone with a hidden disability such as autism, because fundamentally they do not think the same way that we do. It could be said that *neuro-typicals* lack the *theory of mind* to understand how someone on the autism spectrum thinks.

The neurological makeup of individuals on the autism spectrum makes it difficult for them to integrate the various elements of a social interaction into a "big picture," which impacts their ability to develop the people skills needed to navigate the social demands of the workplace. Many individuals on the spectrum want to interact with others, but they do not know how. They can experience deep feelings, but because of their challenges it may appear otherwise. They may feel empathy, but not be able to express it.

To successfully manage employees on the spectrum, it is essential that we learn to view the world from their perspective—and we hope this book will play a large part in expanding your awareness of the difficulties these individuals face. In this chapter, we will discuss the neurological and cognitive differences of individuals on the autism spectrum that contribute to their social challenges in the workplace, including difficulty understanding nonverbal cues and office politics, interpreting figurative language, and problems "fitting in."

On a positive note:

- Employees on the spectrum are loyal and honest, with a strong sense of social justice and a tendency to speak their mind.

As you read this chapter, please remember that not all individuals with autism will display all of the behaviors discussed. Each individual on the spectrum is different, and their challenges related to autism will be unique to them.

Section 6.1: Does he even care?

Topics covered

- Does not make eye contact

- Seems bored or uninterested

- Speaks in a monotone, too loudly, or too quickly

- Never remembers anyone's name or face

- Seems self-centered, rude, or oblivious to others' feelings

Are you seeing these behaviors?

- You are delivering a performance review to one of your employees, but when you are finished, he looks at the ceilings, says "Are you done?" and leaves the room. *And you think to yourself, "Does he even care?"*

- While explaining the details of a project to a colleague, he stares blankly at the toes of his shoes.

- An employee smiles excessively during a meeting for no apparent reason.

What are the underlying issues?
Empathy and the workplace

"I don't read people very well, so I don't know what they need."

Empathy is the concern we feel in response to our awareness of the feelings and needs of another person. This ability to "put ourselves in another person's shoes" allows us to relate to the thoughts, emotions, or experience of others. In the workplace, empathy also translates to having respect for one's colleagues and reflects the ability to connect with them. Individuals on the spectrum may relate to their co-workers in a brusque or dismissive way, appear to be bored or uninterested, intolerant of the ideas of others, and oblivious to another person's feelings, so we assume that they lack empathy. However, this is not the case. People with autism do not lack the *capacity* to care about other people's feelings and often care very much about connecting with others. They do, however, have difficulty identifying the emotions they observe in other people and knowing how to respond appropriately.

What we think of as *empathy* is actually made up of two components. *Cognitive empathy* is associated with theory of mind, and refers to identifying what is going on in another person's mind through interpreting facial expressions, tone of voice, and language used, against the backdrop of the context of a situation. *Emotional empathy* allows a person to use this information to imagine what that person is feeling and then care about it and respond appropriately. While individuals on the spectrum may have more difficulty than the average person understanding someone else's perspective (cognitive empathy), once they are made aware of it, they do have the capacity to care about how that person feels (emotional empathy).[23] In short, they may have the desire to reach out, comfort, or help another person, but in a given situation they may not know how and consequently do nothing or do the wrong thing.

Although reacting empathically to the emotional state of another person might seem intuitive, it depends on several processes. For example, when you notice that a colleague is upset, theory of mind helps you understand what they are feeling (rather than experience the same intensity of emotion yourself), and you respond by feeling in tune and expressing concern that is appropriate to the situation. The response of an employee on the spectrum, however, may seem detached or insensitive, or they may simply walk away; yet family and friends of individuals with autism often say that they "feel too much." Current research suggests that both observations may be true. Individuals with autism may notice that a person is emotional, but because of impairments with theory of mind, they may not understand what that emotion means or be able to regulate their internal reaction to it; they may become so overwhelmed by the other person's emotional state that they withdraw, thus appearing cold or uncaring.[24, 25]

Making or maintaining eye contact

The eyes are central to nonverbal communication and reveal a great deal about what we are really thinking and feeling from moment to moment. In our society, eye contact indicates someone's involvement and attention. The ability to "look someone in the eye" suggests trust and truthfulness; and in the business world, establishing eye contact shows confidence.

Many individuals on the autism spectrum have trouble making or maintaining eye contact, which is often interpreted as a sign of laziness, dishonesty, or lack of interest. Overall, it is important to keep in mind that individuals on the spectrum are not avoiding eye contact as a choice, but rather because of a neurological difference. Facial expressions constantly change during communication, so people with autism may find them distracting and difficult to follow. Some may find it painful to maintain eye contact, because doing so makes them anxious.

"If somebody requests that I look in their eye, I'm going to be filled with anxiety. I'm also going to lose focus about what I'm supposed to be discussing."

People with autism say that they can either think and respond or look someone in the eyes—it is literally one of those options. Recent research suggests that we operate the same way: our brains have a difficult time thinking complex thoughts while constantly maintaining eye contact,[26] so we switch between looking at someone to show we are engaged, and looking away in order to concentrate while explaining something complicated. Keep in mind, not every situation warrants extended eye contact: social convention in New York City results in eye contact that averages less than two seconds![27]

A colleague with autism may respond to a request for eye contact by unintentionally staring, which can be misinterpreted as an affront or a challenge of authority.

"I knew that you were supposed to make eye contact, although the result of that is that I may have stared too intensely."

Employees on the spectrum should never be forced to have direct eye contact; however, they can learn to give the *impression* of eye contact by focusing on more neutral parts of the face, such as the nose or glasses, or by using reports, memos, and other visual materials as a common focal point while discussing a project.

Facial expressions

"Sometimes it looks as if I'm either not paying attention or I'm being dishonest—neither of which is the case. I'm just thinking about what the appropriate response is, or what's the answer, the solution to the problem posed."

As previously discussed, a large component of empathy is our ability to decipher the meaning of facial expressions, tone and inflections in the voice, and body language. Much of our social development involves learning to understand the needs and feelings of others through observing the subtle differences among the thousands of combinations of facial expressions and tone of voice.

We also use these same tools to signal our own thoughts and feelings in response to others. Facial expressions are remarkably similar across different cultures, and our ability to use them to spontaneously express our feelings is largely innate. However, the lack of eye contact of individuals on the spectrum may make it difficult for them to learn which facial expressions are deemed suitable for various situations. Additionally, they may exhibit inappropriate or unusual facial expressions, such as excessive smiling, in response to anxiety or a scowl in large group meetings where they feel uncomfortable.

A common complaint of co-workers is that a request or explanation is met with a blank expression, which makes a person on the spectrum seem detached, uninterested, or uncomprehending. Keep in mind that for these individuals, processing social interactions may require a lot of cognitive power. As a result, they may have difficulty reacting while they are trying to understand what you are saying, or they may need time to decide on the correct response to your request.

Voice quality

Meaning in verbal communication is a combination of *what* is said (the actual words) as well as *how* it is said. Intonation, inflection, and rhythm comprise the musicality of speech, which conveys social cues such as emotion and intent. Not surprisingly, individuals with autism generally have difficulty decoding the nuances of speech in others, which can in turn impact their own vocal expressiveness. While people with autism have normal or highly developed language skills, they may speak in a monotone without inflection, as though the emotional content is absent, or their speech may lack a natural rhythm. Feedback throughout their lives may have made them aware of how they sound, although it may not be under their control. If a person speaks too quickly, too softly, or too loudly, he may respond to reminders, such as asking him to bring down his voice if it is too loud, or if he is going from a noisy setting to a quiet one.

Recognizing faces and remembering names

> *"For me, not remembering faces is embarrassing and a big part of some of the issues that I struggle with."*

> *"I continuously embarrass myself by calling someone Bob or John, when their name is Margaret or Joseph."*

People like to be remembered, and the ability to recognize colleagues and clients and recall specific facts about them is a key component of many jobs. Although individuals with autism show remarkable memory for detailed information, many have difficulty remembering faces. We generally recognize a face by recalling a combination of facial elements, such as the type of eyes, shape of the nose, and so on. A person on the spectrum, however, might store facial information as unconnected details, rather than the configuration of a specific "face," and consequently have difficulty recognizing that face in the future.[28] They often rely on hairstyles, glasses, and clothing to identify colleagues and might be confused when another person shares some of those same characteristics or those details change. An individual on the spectrum may associate a co-worker with a specific context (such as department where the person works) and may not recognize that person when encountered outside of the workplace.

"I tell people that if I run into you on the street next week and have no idea who you are, please do not be offended."

Rudeness

"When I get tired, my filter doesn't work so well. So sometimes what I'm thinking comes out and it shouldn't…it's not intended to offend anybody, it just is."

Polite behavior also requires the ability to filter what is on one's mind, but an individual with autism might "think out loud" and not be aware that what he says might be offensive.

The way most people process language is different from individuals on the spectrum, who tend to be literal in their thinking. This processing difference, combined with the tendency to be very direct, may make individuals on the spectrum come across as being rude, curt, or taciturn. Most people are concerned about the impression they make on others, and learn that a little bit of tact in the workplace goes a long way when expressing one's opinion. Someone on the spectrum, however, may consider his observations and opinions to be obvious; although others may find his comments or abrupt responses rude or insensitive, the individual may feel that he is merely "stating a fact."

A colleague with autism may want to connect socially, but may not know how, often "downloading data" on colleagues rather than engaging in a two-way conversation. Social dialogue requires an organized give-and-take: one person receives information from another person, processes it, responds appropriately, waits for the next response or piece of information, and so on. This often presents challenges for individuals on the spectrum, who struggle with simultaneously understanding the meaning of what they hear, while determining the correct response to it. When a conversation goes into unfamiliar territory, they may feel unable to contribute and may try to turn the conversation back into the comfort zone of their own interests or abruptly end the conversation.

What can you do about an employee who doesn't seem to care?

A key to successfully managing employees on the spectrum is to keep in mind that their behavior is largely based on how their brains work—they are not intentionally trying to alienate people by avoiding eye contact, hijacking a conversation, or being rude. Quite the contrary, they are often very desirous of making a connection with others, and know that they struggle in doing so.

It is important to provide *context* while pointing out inappropriate behavior. A simple, clear, and direct explanation of *why* certain behaviors may be considered rude or insensitive and *how* the recipient might feel will be appreciated and allow the individual to expand his repertoire of appropriate responses in various workplace situations. You can bridge the gap between how he thinks and how his behavior might be perceived by others by explaining why certain behaviors are generally interpreted negatively.

If an employee that is disclosed seems rude or acts inappropriately, speak with him about what might be *behind* these behaviors. Are they experiencing challenges or anxieties related to autism? Are they having issues interacting with certain colleagues? Are situations on the job or outside of work influencing their behavior? Some facial expressions that seem inappropriate, such as smiling excessively, may be related to anxiety.

The inability of people on the spectrum to decode facial expressions, vocal tone, and body language can leave them largely unaware of what a colleague may be thinking and feeling, and they may not know what to say or how to respond appropriately. Keeping in mind that his intention is not to offend, you can take the employee aside and coach him on how he might rephrase something, so it is less offensive to his colleagues. If the individual repeatedly makes the same mistake, a manager can point to the similarities in these situations and suggest, "Would you like me to write down a better way to say it, so you can practice?"

It may be easier for some colleagues with autism to communicate *without* eye contact, so never force them to look at you directly, and give an extra beat of time for them to look away while they gather their thoughts to respond. If necessary, you can suggest a way for them to casually explain this to others, such as, "When you ask me a question, I may not look at you when I'm thinking of a response, because I think better if I'm able to look elsewhere."

If the individual is dealing with clients, suggest looking at a more neutral part of the face, such as the nose or glasses, to give the impression of eye contact, or use something visual, such as a report or list, to create a common focal point. Sometimes the request for eye contact results in excessive staring, so suggest that he occasionally break the stare by focusing on the shoulder of the other person.

Recognizing faces and remembering names can also be a challenge for someone on the spectrum. If your company does not have a corporate directory with photos, you can suggest that he maintain a list of people and identifying characteristics on the computer or a smartphone for quick access. If he has difficulty distinguishing between members of his team, he can ask if they will let him take their photos to add to a contact list on his phone. Prior to meeting with clients or new staff, prepare the employee by providing names and distinguishing characteristics, such as hair color, height, and obvious facial features.

When giving direction or explanations, we are used to receiving feedback from the other person, such as nodding, saying "OK," and so on. Keep in mind that although an individual with autism may remain silent and look at you blankly or not at all, he may actually be listening intently, so give him a moment to process what you are saying. Asking "Do you understand?" is not sufficient and will most likely be answered "Yes," so confirm that you have been understood by asking him to repeat what you have said.

Related material

- Chapter 5: Talking

Section 6.2: He thinks he knows it all!

Topics covered

- Sees everything as black and white
- Always corrects others
- Always needs to be right
- Needs to do things HIS way
- Cannot accept criticism of his work
- Speaks in a stilted or an overly formal fashion

Are you seeing these behaviors?

- After asking an employee to make a list of changes to a report, you receive a six-page memo outlining why the report is "ridiculous." *And you think to yourself, "He thinks he knows it all!"*

- A colleague repeatedly interrupts a conversation to correct someone on minor facts.

- An employee proposes a solution during a team meeting, but becomes very defensive when colleagues question some minor points.

What are the underlying issues?

While individuals on the spectrum typically have difficulty understanding how people think and feel, they bring to the workplace considerable expertise in very specialized areas of knowledge. They do, however, have a specific way of thinking. As "literal thinkers" they tend to be very detail-oriented and logical, with the ability to acquire and store many pieces of information as well as recognize complex patterns and irregularities in data or procedures. By contrast, "abstract thinkers" are more conceptual, focusing on the "big picture" rather than the details, and are more able to deal with ambiguity and change.

Sharing their knowledge and using it to solve problems is not only a source of pride for people on the spectrum but also a means to communicate. However, this can backfire due to their inability to "read" people and situations. They may be perceived as overbearing, arrogant, and inflexible "know-it-alls" who correct others and insist on doing things *their* way. On the other hand, their subject matter expertise and logical thought process can be a great asset to colleagues who take the time to understand how they think.

"If somebody else had difficulty or a problem with a technical issue, I actually had a reputation for being somebody that people

would come to, and I would sit down and help them figure out and fix the problem."

Black-and-white thinking

Literal thinkers tend to view the world in terms of "black and white" or "right and wrong." For example, a colleague with autism might rigidly adhere to written policies and procedures, even if others have found a faster way to accomplish a task. They consider information, procedures, and their own observations as "fact" and therefore not subject to interpretation.

"It's very hard in a work setting to not see the world as black and white. If someone says, 'I have another idea,' and that idea doesn't fit into my black-and-white thinking, I won't like that idea."

The quick pace of project deadlines may sometimes require a deviation from an established rule or method. People with autism often think that there is only one "right" way to do something, so being asked to do it differently is one of their biggest workplace challenges, especially if they are uncomfortable with change in general. Refusing a manager's request to take a shortcut on an established procedure to move a project along is often perceived as being stubborn, difficult, or negative. Theory of mind is a factor in these situations: an employee with autism cannot anticipate the manager's needs, so "No" is often a defense mechanism for the anxiety of not understanding the manager's perspective or reasons for modifying the procedure.

Being right

Individuals on the spectrum tend to place a great deal of importance on accuracy, are excellent at finding errors, and like to share this knowledge. Unfortunately, this sharing of knowledge can come across as constant correcting of others and be perceived as quite annoying, particularly when the point they are making is irrelevant or insignificant, such as insisting during a lunchtime conversation that a colleague refer to a tomato as a "fruit" instead of a "vegetable."

Employees with autism may not understand that most people do not like being corrected, especially in front of others. It is usually not their intention to annoy or insult, but rather to point out what they consider to be obvious. However, an individual on the spectrum may be perceived as condescending, especially if he speaks in a stilted or professorial manner, uses esoteric language, or brags about an accomplishment because he considers it a fact.

Because of their attention to detail, employees with autism are often the ones to identify mistakes in data or procedure, but may report it without regard for someone's feelings or position. Sometimes the issue is not a question of *whether* they should report errors, but *how* and *to whom*.

"If I saw any kind of a mistake, I would point it out immediately. And it had never occurred to me that this was something that some people might not appreciate, especially if they had anything to do with the error in question."

Individuals with autism may have difficulty entertaining any other viewpoint than their own, especially when it comes to their area of expertise. When asked to try something different, most people can be flexible enough to deal with any problems as they come up. A person on the spectrum, however, may become anxious about the request to "work it out as you go along," because they feel they have not prepared for every scenario, like a computer without adequate programming. Their coping mechanism in response to recommendations is often misinterpreted as hubris: a barrage of questions about "what if" scenarios may appear as a rejection of the idea, when it is actually an attempt to build the "internal flowchart" they need to deal with potential roadblocks.

"You've got to really listen, really have to listen hard, to try not to let your predisposition to have a neat, ordered life interfere with new ideas."

Colleagues with autism are eager to share their expertise, but their lack of context and inflexibility make it difficult for them to understand that skills, abilities, and knowledge exist in varying degrees. When explaining something to a colleague, an employee on the spectrum may have difficulty assessing how much information the colleague already has, and what new information is needed. As a result, he may become impatient when that person does not immediately grasp "the obvious."

"I get annoyed by people who aren't as analytic as me—why don't they see it as clearly as I see it?"

Accepting criticism

Individuals on the spectrum tend to be perfectionists, holding themselves as well as others to the same high standard. This makes them valued contributors at work, because they strive to do the best job possible. However, the black-and-white, all-or-nothing thinking of people on the spectrum may make them anxious if they feel their performance is not perfect. This makes them particularly sensitive to criticism, which they may equate with failure. According to Temple Grandin, an expert in autism who is also on the spectrum:

> They see themselves and the world around them in polar opposites, and this tendency feeds their need to be perfect. Even the tiniest mistakes and mishaps can feel like monumental failures to them, creating high levels of anxiety when their efforts or the events around them do not measure up to this all-or-nothing scale.[29]

How do you deal with an employee who thinks he knows it all?

It is frustrating when an employee or colleague feels he "knows better," but if you take the time to ask, you will often find that individuals on the spectrum will generally have a reasonable explanation for why they do not want to comply with your request. The most important strategy you can have as a manager is to "put yourself in their shoes" and provide context when you ask for changes in procedure. Explain the reasoning behind a shortcut or changes you want to make, then allow the individual to express any concerns he may have—not only will you meet with less resistance, he may suggest a more expedient solution!

Remind the employee upfront that the work he delivers might need to be modified, depending on who will use it and for what purpose, so he is prepared if that happens. Remember that employees on the spectrum are very logical, so take the time to explain your thought process and the outcome you want to achieve. Provide context by explaining, "This is what I was looking for and *why*," or "I have to take your work and use it *here*," rather than, "This isn't what I wanted."

The black-and-white thinking of an employee on the spectrum may limit his understanding that everyone makes mistakes, and that his colleagues generally do not appreciate being corrected publicly. If criticizing colleagues during meetings is an issue, a team leader can request that the individual keep a list of concerns that they can address together after the meeting. A manager can also give a general rule such as "If you think you are seeing a major mistake being made, come and tell me." Keep in mind that individuals on the spectrum are not without feelings, and a reminder such as "Think how you feel when someone corrects you, and you feel you're right" can be very effective.

When an individual on the spectrum finds mistakes, he may feel the need to resolve them immediately. You may need to explain that some mistakes are more important than others, and suggest that he come to you first, if he has difficulty distinguishing between ones that are critical and those that are not.

Perfectionism and difficulties with emotional regulation often make it difficult for individuals on the spectrum to receive criticism or understand that a mistake does not mean that he needs to scrap the entire project. If the work product is not what you were expecting, give the employee examples of what the outcome should look like, and provide him with a peer mentor for interim feedback during the revision process. Making a statement such as "You may feel this work is all wrong, but it's not" followed by feedback that is specific and constructive will help the employee address your concerns and move on.

Similarly, during a performance review, put criticism in context for an individual on the spectrum by first discussing what he does well and how he can build on those strengths. Explain where he needs to make changes and why, and then provide clear guidance on how he can improve. If the employee is disclosed, give him the opportunity to bring up any issues related to autism that may be giving him problems in these areas.

Related material

- Chapter 10: Work Quality

Section 6.3: He doesn't get it!

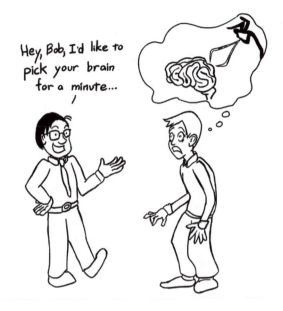

Topics covered

- Interprets everything literally
- Cannot take a hint
- Does not understand jokes or sarcasm
- Does not understand office politics
- Has difficulty working on a team
- Mishandles client interactions

Are you seeing these behaviors?

- After learning that his report is still not finished, you tell an employee, "I suppose I'll just have to do it myself," to which the employee replies, "OK," and walks away. *And you think to yourself, "He doesn't get it!"*

- An employee constantly drops by the CEO's office, taking the company's "open door" policy for suggestions to heart.

- An employee must repeatedly be reminded to not "cc" emails to the entire department.

What are the underlying issues?

Human communication is constant and complex. According to psychologist and science journalist Daniel Goleman:

> Even though we can stop talking, we cannot stop sending signals (our tone of voice, our fleeting expressions) about what we feel. Even when people try to suppress all signs of their emotions, feelings have a way of leaking anyway. In this sense, when it comes to emotions, we cannot **not** communicate.[30]

Theory of mind helps us interpret the endless stream of cues that signal what someone is thinking. However, people don't always say what they mean or act the way we expect. To individuals with autism, the unpredictable nature of human behavior conflicts with their view of the world: a collection of absolute rules, logical systems, order, and facts. Despite their best efforts, as soon as they learn one rule of behavior, another situation seems to go against it.

It is impossible for us to catalog every combination of facial expression, vocal inflection, and language, so we rely on our instinct, judgement, and experience to interpret the many aspects of social situations. We notice their relative "sameness," which allows us to generalize appropriate behavior over a wide range of contexts. Discerning the differences in social contexts helps us learn that appropriate behavior in one situation may not translate to another.

However, this is not the norm for individuals with autism, whose inability to "read" people and the context of social situations often leaves them feeling like they are in a foreign country, trying to understand the rules and behavior of its inhabitants without a translator or guide. As a result, they typically interpret common expressions literally, have difficulty deciphering sarcasm and jokes, fail to pick up on social cues, and seem oblivious to the politics of the workplace.

Literal thinking and figurative language

"Idioms and expressions are a struggle for me."

Many of the expressions you hear throughout the workday are not meant to be taken literally, yet we know what they mean, such as "Let's put a pin in that discussion" or "We need to be on the same page."

Understanding figurative language involves going beyond the *literal* meaning of the words and interpreting the *intended* meaning within the context of the situation; for example, assessing what the message is about rather than focusing on what the message literally says. Without understanding the intention or perspective of the person speaking (theory of mind), an individual with autism will be confused by a phrase that seems unrelated to the conversation.

Many people on the spectrum think literally, so the figurative language that we use in the workplace presents a challenge to them. They process words at their face value and have difficulty understanding the shifting meanings of *sarcasm* and *idioms*, such as "thinking outside of the box" (because an actual box has nothing to do with the process of thinking). Similarly, a *rhetorical question* does not require an answer: when you say "Would you mind pulling together the sales figures?" you are politely assigning a task, not asking for someone's feeling on the matter. A colleague with autism, however, may interpret "would you mind?" literally, and might answer honestly, "Yes" or "No," without registering that he is to compile the sales figures.

"'Thinking out of the box'—I have absolutely no idea what that meant."

We use figurative language in the workplace as a shortcut, and rely on the context in which it is used to understand the speaker's intent. Here are some examples of common business idioms that individuals on the spectrum find confusing:

- "The ball is in your court."

- "We need to be on the same wavelength."

- "Don't talk shop at the lunch with Mr. Jones."

- "Pick his brain about the merger."

- "Bring me up to speed on the project."

Most likely you instantly got the gist of the above phrases, but you might need to ask someone what they meant by "Throw the database project over the wall"[31] or "Give the analysis some stick."[32] An individual on the spectrum, however, may hesitate to ask for clarification, because he does not want to seem incompetent.

Imprecise directions can also cause confusion. For example, "Go over those figures *later*" could mean in an hour, a day, or a week, but most people interpret the request based on past experience and the context of the situation. An individual with autism, however, needs to be told exactly *when*, *how*, and *how much* he needs to do, so he can focus on the task rather than the interpretation.

Literal thinking is related to the "black-and-white" thinking discussed earlier in this chapter. Most of us think in terms of "shades of gray," such as when we apply the same rule or procedure to a current situation that is *similar* but not *identical* to one we have encountered in the past. However, an employee on the spectrum may have difficulty knowing how to proceed when instructed to do a task "the same way as last time" if the situation is not exactly the same. Being specific about what procedures will stay the same, while pointing out what may be different, will not only clarify what he needs to do, but also help him learn how to approach similar tasks in the future.

Sarcasm and jokes

"Someone will say a joke and I won't get it—everyone's laughing, and I'll be confused."

When you hear a joke or sarcasm, you must integrate multiple channels of input: the *meaning* of the words, the *context* of the situation, the *intent* of the speaker, and, in the case of a joke, the *mindset* of the central characters. All of these depend on theory of mind and therefore can be difficult for those on the spectrum to understand. Sarcastic comments such as "That was fun!" after a long, difficult meeting may be particularly perplexing to someone with autism, since the positive words spoken do not match the negative tone of voice and facial expression.

Because they take words at face value, people on the spectrum may have a difficult time determining if someone is teasing, or they may misinterpret the tone of an email. This is not so unusual: the need to distinguish between joking and serious statements in casual online communication was the driving factor in the invention of "emoticons" like the ubiquitous "smiley face."[33]

People with autism do not lack the *capacity* to make jokes, appreciate wordplay, or see the humor in a situation, although they may have difficulty processing more complex forms of jokes told around the water cooler, which tend to be embedded in social context. Humor involves thinking about something with a different twist, and their unusual way of viewing things can be humorous, although some of the jokes they tell may be funny only to themselves. Nonetheless, some individuals on the spectrum have an excellent sense of humor that they are happy to share.

"Often we would have a going away lunch for somebody who was leaving the company, and I actually became known as the person who would make the funny speech."

Social cues

The over 40 muscles in the face can form thousands of facial expressions, and for individuals on the spectrum, the face is a confusing array of motion: eyebrows move up and down, the mouth assumes a myriad of shapes and the eyes narrow or open wide. While they may understand the most basic facial expressions used in conversation, they often cannot read signs of impatience, boredom, or frustration. They may be oblivious to cues signaling that they are standing too close in conversation or talking too loudly. As a result, individuals with autism may not stop behaviors, such as talking or interrupting, in spite of being given strong nonverbal cues to do so, or they may ask questions that seem obvious or extraneous.

> *"It's difficult for me to read a person's face, so I've come to learn that, through asking questions, you understand how a person's feeling more so than just trying to read their physical posture or their body language."*

The ability to decipher facial expressions, tone of voice, and gestures as well as use them to express oneself is essential for effective communication. For many individuals with autism, the avoidance of eye contact impacts their ability to read faces and social cues, so receiving and expressing nonverbal communication presents a continuous challenge for them and their colleagues. By observing the eyes and faces of others, we learn to use the nuances of our own body language to reflect what we are thinking; this happens spontaneously and with little effort on our part. The muscles of the eyes, in particular, are finely tuned to express feelings. However, individuals with autism tend to avoid eye contact and therefore miss critical information, not only about the other person, but about facial expressions in general. Because they lack these reference points, facial expressions of people on the spectrum are sometimes considered inappropriate, blank, or hard to interpret.

Honesty

Lying is part of the *hidden curriculum* and requires a complicated cognitive process of creating a credible lie, while withholding part of the truth. These mental gymnastics elude most individuals on the autism spectrum, who tend to be honest and truthful. A "white lie" is occasionally used in the workplace to circumvent an awkward situation or avoid hurt feelings, and we often "filter" what we say in order to achieve an end goal. For example, a team leader may not mention the problematic aspect of a project, to keep people focused on priorities, while an executive in the midst of a negotiation may decide that not all things need to be disclosed up front. Even if they do understand the need for withholding the truth, doing so is likely to make an individual on the spectrum very uncomfortable. Scientist Temple Grandin (who is on the spectrum) describes the anxiety resulting from trying to keep one's world in order if there is false data in it:

> I become extremely anxious when I have to tell a little white lie on the spur of the moment. To be able to tell the smallest fib, I have to rehearse it many times in my mind. I run video simulations of all the different things the other person might ask. If the other person comes up with an unexpected question, I panic.[34]

As discussed previously, individuals on the spectrum are often considered rude, because they tend to bluntly state what they consider to be true. On the other hand, they are generally not offended when receiving straightforward feedback from others, and do not need the "verbal niceties" or "sugar coating" that we often employ to spare someone's feelings:

> *"Tell me what's going on, don't sugar coat it. Tell me the truth—I will work on it and accommodate it."*

Keep in mind that the inherent honesty of a colleague with autism can be a benefit in the workplace: if you ask his opinion on a project or procedure, you will most likely get an honest and direct answer!

Individuals on the spectrum assume that since they are truthful, other people are as well, so an employee may not notice when people are lying or being insincere. Unfortunately, the trusting nature of individuals with autism can make them easy to manipulate and the target of bullies.

> *"One of the traits of Asperger's is basically I believe what anyone says. So, if someone is not really telling me the truth, or using a social setting kind of skill, I don't understand that."*

Office politics

> *"The politics that I miss, I really miss."*

Many aspects of office politics are socially determined and present challenges for people with autism:

- What is the chain of command for addressing work-related issues?

- Who do you "cc" on an email?

- Who gets rewarded and for what?

Every company has an official organizational chart, but many companies also have an unofficial or unwritten chain of command that reflects the actual structure of power and decision-making in each department. While most employees quickly learn who to approach for guidance, whose requests have priority, who to email about project updates, and who has the final say on a project, the individual with autism may find this confusing.

The style of management of some companies is less hierarchical and more matrix-structured and cooperative in nature. Employees from one department often work on projects managed by people from other departments, creating a chain of command that is confusing to many individuals on the spectrum. For example, an accountant working on an interdepartmental project may not know whether to report to his manager in the accounting department or the team leader.

"A middle manager like me can have a really difficult time without a chain of command, without reporting relationships that are clear."

As mentioned previously, individuals with autism have difficulty recognizing the similarities and differences in social situations that determine appropriate behavior, which is further complicated by the various levels of authority in a typical workplace. For example, an employee may not realize that the topics he discusses with his colleagues in casual conversation might not be appropriate when addressing a managing director, or that someone senior does not like to be corrected in an open forum.

Understanding the office dynamic around why a rule may apply to a colleague but not to someone higher up can also be a challenge. The unwritten rules for who gets rewarded or punished and for what type of behavior may be confusing to employees on the spectrum, who take great pride in their work and believe strongly in a meritocracy. Employees with autism are motivated by doing a good job, and sometimes their perceived naivete around office politics results in assignment of more than their fair share of work or unfair treatment in other ways:

> *"Being appreciated and being recognized for my work were important. And probably the most horrible experiences that I had in over my entire 28-year career were one or two occasions when I was deliberately not given credit for something that I had done."*

Working with teams

Teams are the backbone of the modern workplace, whether in person or virtual. Team members have a shared goal and depend on each other to ensure the success of a project. Some teams are highly structured, although many are not, relying on the cooperation of team members to fulfill the needs of the project from their area of expertise as well as support the team's efforts in general.

Participation in teamwork can be challenging to employees with autism, who have difficulty anticipating the needs of one person, let alone several. Extreme attention to detail and perfectionism can affect the speed at which a team member with autism completes assigned project tasks, as he can struggle with initiating and organizing an assignment in general. He may balk at taking on a task that he believes is irrelevant or when he feels that other team members are not doing their fair share of the work (these issues are covered in depth in Part Three: Work Performance).

> *"I have difficulty working in a team. I'm not very good at being the person who's supposed to facilitate and when there is no clear person who is supposed to distribute the work, it's very difficult to figure out who to listen to, what to do."*

The members of teams in today's businesses might include individuals from different functional areas, different geographic locations, or employees from the client side. In general, people on the spectrum have difficulties with change of any kind, and variations in the composition of the team or meeting times and locations may cause anxiety or be met with resistance. They may find the lack of a clear chain of command confusing, as well as shifting priorities between groups.

> *"As far as meetings were concerned, they ranged from bearable to absolute torture. The one exception to that being, if the meeting was a purely technical discussion, where we were just hashing out technical issues, then I had a great time."*

Teams depend on meetings, and the fluid exchange of ideas often presents a challenge to individuals on the spectrum, who have difficulty processing the discussion of issues that are not technical in nature or are outside of their exact area of expertise. Employees with autism add value to a team by drawing from a highly specialized knowledge base, and their problem-solving nature can lead to innovative solutions. However, an individual on the spectrum values what he sees as fact over tact, and his assessment may be a blunt, "No, we shouldn't do it that way," or "You're making a big mistake," and he may refuse to drop the subject once the meeting has moved to other issues.

> *"Teamwork's very hard. I don't read people very well, and teamwork requires that you understand the other person's need, trying to fill that need, even if they don't specifically say it."*

As office politics are not part of the mindset of an individual on the spectrum, assessment of a process or procedure is generally without bias. A research study of managers of employees with Asperger Syndrome conducted at the UK's Nottingham Business School concluded:

> While criticism is unlikely to be universally welcomed, line managers appreciated having a team member who was willing to criticize or point out problems with a particular decision or

process, or ask questions and articulate complaints that others may be afraid or embarrassed to raise.[35]

Interactions with clients

"There's really not a difference between building a relationship at work or with a client. It still requires you get a connection to somebody, and it's very hard for people to connect with me, and me to connect with people."

Meeting clients presents challenges for individuals with autism, as different rules may be in play than in the day-to-day workplace, including what to wear, how much to say about the status of a project, or how much socialization is required. Some employees on the spectrum are very social and outgoing, and they might interact well with clients, if they are provided clear rules about boundaries and how they should escalate issues or client-related matters. Other individuals may be overly social, and their excessive talking may be counterproductive. In contrast, some individuals on the spectrum may not be comfortable at all with the level of social interaction required and become very anxious. Making the decision to place an employee with autism in a client-facing role should be dealt with on a person-by-person basis.

Issues often arise when an employee on the spectrum is required to work at a client's workplace. An employee who is disclosed may have learned to be successful in his own workplace, because his managers and colleagues have become adept at providing the accommodations he needs. However, the individual's issues may resurface if he is required to work in an unfamiliar environment.

An individual on the spectrum with highly developed technical skills may not be suitable for a business management role, but he may do well on a client team that requires more technical collaboration than socialization. Obviously, it is best if your client company understands autism, and the employee is disclosed, so you can discuss with the client how best to integrate the employee when he is on-site. For example, matching a systems engineer on the spectrum with peers in the same technical area at the client's workplace will allay the individual's anxiety about interacting socially, while giving him the opportunity to add value to the client by providing specialized technical support and expertise.

How do you deal with an employee who "doesn't get it"?

When dealing with a person on the spectrum, always keep in mind that what seems obvious to you is precisely that—obvious to *you*! The subtle messages conveyed by facial expressions, tone of voice, and body language are difficult for individuals on the spectrum to interpret. Just as with social situations, the key to communicating with a colleague on the spectrum about any topic is to be direct, detailed, and specific, without relying on body language, tone of voice, or sarcasm to convey your meaning. Say what you mean in straightforward language, rather than using business jargon, idioms, or sarcasm.

An individual with autism needs to be told exactly *when, how,* and *how much* you want him to do, so he can focus on the task rather than the interpretation. This requires being specific about project due dates and requirements, and, if possible, providing examples of similar completed assignments, research, or reports so the desired outcome and format is clear (these issues are covered in depth in Part Three: Work Performance). Table 6.1 lists a few examples of how you might restate some common workplace requests so that they more directly communicate what you mean.

Table 6.1: Common business idioms restated

Commonly said	Direct restatement
Can you take care of this report now?"	"I would like you to stop working on what you are doing and do this report first, then finish the other project."
"I need you to think outside of the box."	"I would like you to come up with some ideas that are different than the ones we have been using."
"Kick it upstairs."	"Forward it, or pass it on to your supervisor."

"Yes" or "No" questions such as "Do you understand me?" can be too vague for a person on the spectrum, who will likely answer "Yes" whether he has grasped your meaning or not, because he does not want to seem incompetent. Always take a moment to *check for understanding* by asking the employee to repeat back to you his interpretation of what he heard you say. Keep in mind that an individual on the spectrum relies on asking questions to understand what another person needs, so give more clarification if he requests it and understand that he may need to hear the answer more than once.

Giving direct but respectful feedback to individuals with autism is not offensive; it is good management and will be appreciated. If an employee has crossed a line with you or a colleague, keep in mind that he may not be aware of the effect of his behavior, and may be surprised to learn that he offended someone. Most people on the spectrum shut down when they are in the presence of strong emotions, so always give feedback in a calm manner. Acknowledge your feelings within the *context* of the situation by explaining how his behavior *in that situation* affected the person on the receiving end, and then suggest how he might have acted more appropriately.

When you notice that an employee with autism is missing subtle cues from a co-worker, intervene with a direct explanation, such as "Bob seems to be busy right now, so you can talk about this later." If the employee is disclosed, you can explain to colleagues how they can set limits or directly cue the individual when "he doesn't take a hint."

Some individuals on the spectrum understand sarcasm and jokes, but many do not. If you are working with someone who really does not understand sarcasm, then avoid using it with that individual. He also may be confused by what others consider "teasing" and feel very uncomfortable being the focus of it—intervene if necessary. Keep in mind that using sarcasm in the workplace with an individual who clearly has difficulty understanding it might fall into the realm of bullying.

The chain of command must be clearly specified for an individual with autism to succeed in the workplace. Clarify who he needs to ask for time off, who he should approach for help and guidance on various projects, and the protocol for volunteering for projects or doing non-work-related activities in the office.

An individual on the spectrum needs clear rules of engagement within the office, especially as it pertains to office politics and working on a team. He may have difficulty holding on to a thought until someone has finished speaking and might constantly interrupt a meeting to ask questions, so ask him to keep a list of questions for later discussion. Modeling the way to reframe criticism, report mistakes or voice one's opinion in a less combative, more positive way can help an employee on the spectrum get his idea across without offending or embarrassing other team members (see Table 6.2).

Table 6.2: Negative remarks stated positively

Negative remark	Positive version
"You are wrong!"	"I don't see how X will improve Y in your example, so please explain it to me."
"This meeting is a waste of my time!"	"We need to research this idea more fully before we can discuss it properly."
"This report has a lot of stupid mistakes."	"I have a list of things in this report that may not be accurate that I'd like to go over with you."

When working on a team, make sure an employee with autism understands who he should report to for tasks that have been assigned to him, especially if the team members are from different departments or divisions. Clearly outline the requirements, outcomes, and deadlines of tasks in writing, providing specific instructions about *what, how much*, and *when* work is due. Allow the employee's communications to the team to be written as well, and be clear about who should be included on emails.

If you have an employee who has disclosed and who has been successfully integrated into your workplace, it does not necessarily mean that the individual will be suitable for client-facing roles. Some people might do quite well if matched on the client end with employees who do the same type of work, such as actuaries with other actuaries. Other individuals, in their enthusiasm to communicate and connect, may have difficulty with boundaries. Or an employee may be extremely anxious about meeting people that are not part of his workgroup. There's no foolproof way to handle interactions with clients, which is why you don't often see individuals with autism in direct client-facing roles. If it is required that a client meet with the team, sit down with the employee and give a scenario of what it will be like and the specifics of what you expect him to do.

Keep in mind that an employee on the spectrum does not have to give up doing work for a client, although his role may need to be redefined to allow him to work without face-to-face interaction. A manager should set up clear protocols for employees on the spectrum who have interactions with clients, including how to escalate issues and client-related matters, such as "If the client contacts me for anything, I will talk to my supervisor before I respond to him."

Clearly if you are reading this book, you are interested in developing the management strategies to work with people on the spectrum, so that they can be successful employees. However, unless your client understands autism, client-facing roles may be challenging for an employee. If the individual is disclosed, discuss with him what he is comfortable disclosing to the client.

Related material

- Chapter 10: Work Quality

Section 6.4: He doesn't fit in!

Topics covered

- Seems weird and/or irritating
- Cannot understand corporate culture
- Does not adhere to dress code
- Does not participate in office social activities
- Prefers to work alone

Are you seeing these behaviors?

- You have encouraged an employee to socialize more by telling him to sit with his colleagues at lunch. He brings his lunch to their table, and then proceeds to read a book. *And you think to yourself, "He doesn't fit in!"*

- Co-workers complain that an employee is irritating and annoying.

- An employee wears clothing that is mismatched, sloppy, or inappropriate for your workplace.

What are the underlying issues?

Getting along with the people you work with is essential for creating a productive work environment. Coffee breaks, lunches, and "water cooler" conversations all provide colleagues the opportunity to get to know one another outside of meetings and other work-related interactions.

> "The individuals who have founded some of the most successful tech companies are decidedly weird. Examine the founder of a truly innovative company and you'll find a rebel without the usual regard for social customs."[36]

Challenges with social interactions at work often keep employees on the spectrum from "fitting in" with their colleagues, who might describe them as "nerdy," "geeky," or "weird," because the focus and intensity of their interests exceed what is typical. Their way of presenting (e.g. tone of voice, cadence, and volume) can be different; body movements may be odd or clumsy; and facial expressions may not align with the tone of the situation, such as smiling inappropriately during a meeting. Some, but not all individuals on the spectrum, appear a bit "off."

Keep in mind that although some individuals with autism do not have physical manifestations and appear "normal," they may not fit in because of other issues. They may be black-and-white literal thinkers, tend to give too much information, insist on being right and correcting their colleagues, or have problems with organizational skills. An employee on the spectrum who does not appear quirky or weird may still have difficulty fitting in socially at work, because his colleagues often have *higher expectations* for how he should behave.

The context of social interactions in the workplace

"I'm not very good at the small social talk, and I always find myself saying something awkward, so I try not to say things in social settings."

It is not uncommon for an employee on the spectrum to shy away from socializing at work because he finds casual socialization stressful or had negative experiences in the past. He may enjoy lunch with a colleague with whom he feels comfortable, but be unable to handle eating with a group of people. He may want to socialize with co-workers, but his attempts at casual conversation may be awkward or inappropriate.

> *"Going to lunch is my greatest fear. If everybody in the office is going to lunch, and I'm invited, that's the worst thing that could ever happen to me."*

If you are managing someone who is on the spectrum, co-workers may have complained that this person is annoying or irritating. Sometimes the reactions of colleagues are not based on specific incidents, but rather a *combination* of the types of behaviors that have been discussed throughout Part Two, such as interrupting, asking too many questions, talking too much, or fixating on a topic.

The complexity of social situations requires more than knowing *if* a certain behavior is appropriate—you need to know *when* that behavior is appropriate. The *context* of the situation determines which hidden curriculum rules apply, so an individual with autism who has learned a fixed social rule may have difficulty applying or adapting it to the continuously changing context of social interactions.[37] For example, an employee who has learned to participate in casual conversations with colleagues over lunch may be surprised by the negative reaction he receives when talking about his interests during a "working lunch" team meeting.

As one advances up the corporate ladder, the need to interface with more people grows, as does the complexity of office politics and social interactions. Difficulties with "soft skills" and navigating the social landscape of the workplace often keeps an employee on the spectrum from moving to a managerial position or advancing his career in general.

Corporate culture

A company's "culture" provides another type of context: it includes the organization's values, policies, and management style, as well as the nature of the actual work environment. Every company has a culture, but it can vary from a more traditional style with clearly defined hierarchies to a less structured collaborative environment where socialization is expected. Teams may range from several employees within a division to ones that are cross-functional, global, and even virtual.

Individuals with autism tend to be very logical, but the norms of the company's culture and the behavior of co-workers can be as confusing to them as the customs of a foreign country. It is easy to accidentally break a social rule when you do not understand the culture: you would be considered rude if you pointed with your forefinger in Indonesia or made the "OK" sign in Greece![38]

The working environment plays a large part in how successfully an employee on the spectrum integrates into the workplace. If an employee with autism is not comfortable with the amount of socialization in some collaborative environments, he may be better suited to a company culture that is "more work, less play." On the other hand, an employee with a technical background may feel comfortable interacting with other engineers who have a similar way of thinking and working.

Dress code

Like it or not, we are judged by how we dress. A company's "dress code" is part of its culture, and what is considered suitable changes with the type of company. For example, an investment bank generally requires formal business attire, while a t-shirt, jeans, and hoodie are the uniform at many trendy tech firms. The dress code at some workplaces is vague, or very relaxed, or it varies by the type of work, allowing employees to dress more casually while at the office, but requiring a suit and tie when interacting with clients.

An employee on the spectrum may have difficulty deciphering what is considered appropriate to wear. For example, the term "business casual" varies across companies, and the phrase itself is confusing to a literal thinker, because "business" seems the opposite of "casual." He may also see little relationship between what he wears and the quality of his work—after all, Mark Zuckerberg, the founder of Facebook, explained that he wears the same gray t-shirt every day so he can focus his energy on more important business decisions.[39] Additionally, some individuals with autism have sensory issues that make them sensitive to certain fabrics or clothing types, such as collared shirts, neckties, and closed shoes (covered in Part Four: Sensory Issues at Work).

The strain of socializing

For most people, socializing at work is a welcome break that helps them get through the day with less stress and fatigue. For individuals with autism, however, these social interactions may have the opposite effect due to the anxiety created by not understanding social rules of the workplace, such as:

- How much socializing and interaction in the workplace is expected?

- At what times of day can you socialize and with whom?

- What topics of conversation are considered appropriate?

For many employees with autism, the social interactions of the office that we take for granted are fraught with anxiety because of the fear of making mistakes or the repercussions of unintentionally insulting a colleague. People on the spectrum generally have difficulty remaining flexible when things do not go as expected, so an employee may become upset or anxious in social situations when plans change at the last minute.

"I become extremely fatigued from interacting with people by mid-workweek."

According to Temple Grandin, a renowned scientist on the spectrum, "Autistic people tend to be less social. It takes a ton of processor space in the brain to have all the social circuits."[40] By the end of the day, an employee on the spectrum may be drained by the conscious effort required to interact with people. He may avoid participating in additional social activities, so he can re-energize at home and return to work the next day.

How do you deal with an employee who "doesn't fit in"?

Today we live in a culture that celebrates unique personalities, so being quirky or odd does not seem to be much of an issue in many workplaces, especially in the creative and technical fields. However, employees on the spectrum generally stand out because of the degree of eccentricity, as well as the lack of understanding of how their behavior affects their colleagues.

When social problems occur, understanding the perspective of an individual on the spectrum is key in effectively managing the situation. If you ask the employee to describe *what* they did and *what they were thinking* when they did it, you will find in many cases that it is a misunderstanding based on the hidden curriculum. When someone complains that a colleague is "irritating" or "annoying," ask him to describe how and under what circumstances the employee was bothersome, so you can view the behavior in context.

Many of the hidden curriculum rules are not explicitly taught, but are learned through observing the consequences of breaking or maintaining social rules in various settings. While individuals on the spectrum may try to avoid making social mistakes by following explicit rules, they have difficulty generalizing appropriate behavior from one situation to another, because they focus on the *differences* rather than the *similarities* of the circumstances. You can help an employee generalize appropriate behavior across similar situations by describing it in different contexts. For example, when you intervene because an employee with autism persists in correcting others during casual conversations, you can extend the explanation to not correcting someone during a meeting as well.

Most of us spontaneously grasp the context of a situation, such as knowing that conversing with a colleague may be more casual than speaking to a client. People on the spectrum are less aware of how context influences social interactions, so it is important to "push the context button" by pointing out the relevant details of a social situation when explaining *why* certain behaviors were inappropriate, annoying, or unsociable and *how* that behavior affected the other person. Whenever possible, provide an *explicit rule* for the behavior in question that specifies *what*, *when*, *where*, or *how* the rule applies to the situation:

- "Don't comment about someone's personal appearance." (*what*)

- "Wear a shirt and tie when meeting with clients." (*when*)

- "If you get anxious during a meeting, leave the room for a few minutes." (*where*)

- "Correct someone privately, rather than in front of the team." (*how*)

Provide specific guidelines for aspects of the company culture that an employee on the spectrum may find confusing, such as work hours, breaks, and volunteer activities. If necessary, assign a co-worker to act as a reference for questions about office politics, corporate culture, or procedures.

In today's work environment the appropriate wardrobe can be very confusing, especially with a "casual dress" policy, so give clear rules about dress code and grooming standards:

- If you have an environment that requires business attire at all times or a uniform, explain what type of clothing is expected.

- There may be different dress codes for various situations within your workplace. Write them down and give the employee a list of what can be worn in different business scenarios, such as a typical workday, visiting a client on-site, volunteering, or attending a special event.

- In cases where the dress code is casual, but people need to dress up when dealing with clients, give advance notice if possible or instruct the employee to keep a shirt and a tie (men) or skirt and blouse (women) in a desk drawer or closet for a spur-of-the-moment change of clothes.

There are some individuals who have a tremendous sensitivity to certain fabrics, and constricted types of clothing, such as neckties (see Part Four: Sensory Issues at Work). In those situations, to the extent that it can be accommodated, allow them to wear appropriate business attire, with a neatly pressed open-collared dress shirt, minus the tie.

Feel free to invite an individual with autism to join a social activity, but do not take it personally if he declines. When attendance is required (e.g. at a company retreat or group "volunteer" activity), allow more limited participation, if possible.

Some employees on the spectrum are eager to participate in social activities, while others may need to be encouraged. Either way, modeling social situations ahead of time will help the individual be successful. You may need to set boundaries for interacting with senior executives or clients and provide strategies for how to initiate, facilitate, and terminate a conversation, as well as suggest appropriate topics for non-work-related conversations.

People with autism are frequently thought of as loners, but there are many reasons why they may want to spend time away from their colleagues, such as feeling anxious or uncomfortable when socializing, or wanting to focus on their work without interaction or comment from others. Never force the employee to participate; but if he is disclosed, you may ask if there are issues related to autism that are holding him back from socializing, such as becoming fatigued from daily social interactions. Sensory issues may also be in play (covered in Part Four), and the employee may need to have some "down time" because the office environment is too stimulating or a social venue is too noisy.

Related material

- Chapter 11: Emotional Regulation

- Chapter 13: Sensory Overload

Social interaction: Accommodations summary

The *hidden curriculum* is social information that everyone knows without being taught, and it is the basis for many of the social rules in the workplace that are assumed to be understood by all. It involves the deciphering of nonverbal cues such as body language, slang expressions, and subtle social cues, as well as comprehending the meaning of a gesture, facial expression, or tone of voice that does not match what someone says. Understanding the hidden curriculum in the workplace is essential, because it comprises what most people consider to be "polite" behavior and helps employees interpret the demands and expectations of the people with whom they work.

The ability to interact and communicate effectively, pleasantly, and appropriately in social environments is generally referred to as *social intelligence, soft skills*, or *people skills*. Social intelligence requires that you not only imagine *what* another person may be thinking and feeling, but also determine *why* he might have those thoughts and emotions. We get information from a person's facial expressions, body language, and tone of voice as well as the actual words he speaks, and then evaluate how it relates to the current situation, as well as similar situations in the past, and respond accordingly.

Much of this process is spontaneous. We are not consciously aware of how we interpret social cues, understand people's motivations, and respond appropriately, so it is difficult to imagine what life is like for those who do not possess these skills. The neurological makeup of individuals on the autism spectrum makes it difficult for them to integrate the various elements of a social interaction into a "big picture," which impacts their ability to develop the people skills needed to navigate the social demands of the workplace. Many individuals on the spectrum want to interact with others, but they do not know how. They can experience deep feelings, but because of their challenges it may appear otherwise. They may feel empathy, but not be able to express it.

Due to their struggle in deciphering the hidden curriculum of the workplace, common perceptions of employees on the spectrum may be:

- He is rude.

- He thinks he knows it all.

- He misses the subtleties of social cues.

- He doesn't fit in.

> Employees on the spectrum want to integrate successfully into the social fabric of the workplace. Keep in mind that their behavior is largely based on how their brains work—they are not intentionally trying to alienate people by avoiding eye contact, hijacking a conversation, or appearing rude.

Understanding that individuals on the spectrum do not mean to offend, but may need guidance to master the soft skills that come naturally to others, is key in providing constructive coaching to employees and colleagues:

- Provide a simple, clear, and direct explanation of *why* certain behaviors may be considered rude or insensitive and *how* the recipient might feel, when pointing out inappropriate behavior.

- Take the employee aside and coach him on how he might rephrase something so it is less offensive to his colleagues.

Eye contact:

- Never force an employee to look directly at you, as it may be easier for some colleagues with autism to communicate *without* eye contact; give an extra beat of time for them to look away while they gather their thoughts to respond.

- Suggest looking at a more neutral part of the face, such as the nose or glasses, to give the impression of eye contact, or use something visual, such as a report or list, to create a common focal point.

Facial recognition:

- Provide a company directory with photos or suggest an employee maintain a list of people with identifying characteristics on his smartphone for easy reference if he struggles with recognizing faces and remembering names.

Some individuals on the spectrum present as "know-it-alls", never admitting they do not understand something. They may question or criticize all suggestions and respond negatively to critical feedback.

- Confirm that you have been understood by asking the employee to repeat what you have said, rather than just asking "Do you understand me?"

- Explain the reasoning behind a shortcut or changes you want to make, and then allow the individual to express any concerns he may have.

Being critical:

- Request that an employee who is known for frequently correcting others keep a list of mistakes or concerns for sharing privately with his manager.

- Remind individuals who come across as overly critical of others to "Think how you feel when someone corrects you, and you feel you're right."

Accepting criticism:

- Put criticism in context by first discussing what the employee does well and how he can build on those strengths.

- Accompany critical feedback with clear explanations of where he needs to make changes and why, and then provide clear guidance on how he can improve.

Individuals on the spectrum often make social missteps at work because they do not pick up on nonverbal cues, such as body language, tone of voice, or sarcasm.

- Say what you mean in straightforward language, rather than using business jargon, idioms, or sarcasm.

- When you notice that an employee is missing subtle cues from a co-worker, intervene with a direct explanation, such as "Bob seems to be busy right now, so you can talk about this later."

- Give more clarification if requested and understand that an employee on the spectrum may need to hear an answer more than once to process its meaning.

Office politics:

- Specify the chain of command in your workplace.

- Have clear rules of engagement within the office, especially as it pertains to office politics and working on a team.

Client interactions:

- Structure client-facing opportunities for employees on the spectrum to ensure the employee is well matched with the client contact.

- Set up clear protocols for employees on the spectrum who have interactions with clients, including how to escalate issues and client-related matters.

The work day requires social interactions in many different settings, and it can be difficult for an employee on the spectrum to generalize appropriate behavior across similar situations, decipher a corporate culture, or sustain participation in non-work-related events.

- Help an employee understand appropriate social behavior by describing it in different contexts.

- Provide an *explicit rule* for the behavior in question that specifies *what*, *when*, *where*, or *how* the rule applies to the situation whenever possible.

Corporate culture:

- Assign a co-worker to act as a reference (or "go-to" person) for questions about office politics, corporate culture, or procedures.

- Provide specific guidelines for aspects of the company culture that the employee may find confusing, such as work hours, breaks, and volunteer activities.

- Give clear rules about dress code and grooming standards.

Social events:

- Feel free to invite an individual with autism to join a social activity, but do not take it personally if he declines.

- Allow more limited participation, if possible, when attendance is required for mandatory company events such as a company retreat.

- Model social situations, or assign a buddy, ahead of company social events to help the employee be successful.

Part Three

WORK PERFORMANCE

Chapter 7

INTRODUCTION TO WORK PERFORMANCE

In Part Two: Social Issues at Work, we discussed how *theory of mind* (the ability to understand another person's perspective) and the *hidden curriculum* (social rules that have not been explicitly taught, but everyone knows) play a large part in the development of *social skills* or *social intelligence*; issues in these two areas account for many of the difficulties people on the autism spectrum have in social interactions at work. *Context* or seeing the "big picture" has a large role as well, as it gives meaning to the nature of different social situations, allowing an individual to know how to behave appropriately under changing conditions.

In addition to social issues, individuals with autism may struggle with organization, planning and setting priorities, managing time, and remaining flexible and even-keeled when things change unexpectedly. These challenges are related to the group of mental processes called *executive functioning skills* or *organizational skills* that allow us to control and regulate other abilities and behaviors. They are necessary for goal-directed behavior, as they allow us to anticipate outcomes and adapt to changing situations.

Executive functioning

Executive functioning is an umbrella term for the cognitive processes that help us manage and control our thoughts and actions (see Table 7.1). Executive functioning skills are not directly related to IQ, but rather to how well we use the intelligence that we have—like the "absent-minded professor" who can solve complex equations but cannot find anything in his office. As we grow and mature, our executive functioning skills develop to allow us to complete both the simplest and most complex tasks in life.

Table 7.1: Executive functioning skills

PLAN Organize thoughts and materials Prioritize	MANAGE TIME Estimate and allocate time needed Adjust processing speeds
FOCUS Follow through and complete tasks Avoid distractions and shift attention	RETRIEVE INFORMATION Remember details Draw on past learning
REMAIN FLEXIBLE Transition between tasks Cope with changes in routine	REGULATE EMOTIONS Manage frustration and emotions Think before speaking

Other cognitive processes related to work performance are processing speed, focus, and the concept of time. *Processing speed* is not the same as intelligence, but it does affect our ability to complete tasks efficiently. While fast processing speed allows you to sort through information quickly, slower processing speed may result in having trouble carrying out instructions when told to do more than one thing at once; needing more time to make simple decisions or give answers; and keeping up with the give and take of conversations. Regulating processing speed allows you to decide how slowly or quickly to perform a task based upon its priority and the time available.

The *concept of time* includes understanding the passage of time—how much time is needed to complete a task, as well as how much time has elapsed as you work on it. *Time management* is an important component of work performance; how you tackle a task that is due in an hour is different from how you would manage an assignment that is due in two weeks. *Focus*, or the ability to maintain attention on a task, is a key aspect of work performance as well.

Any employee may need help with the various areas of executive functioning, and certainly there is no shortage of business books, coaches, and workshops to strengthen organizational skills in general. However, for individuals with autism, difficulties in executive functioning challenges may be compounded by issues in *other* areas, such as theory of mind, and they may require assistance and accommodations that can specifically address these issues.

Work performance, the "big picture," and theory of mind

In addition to executive functioning skills, the concept of work performance includes specific aspects of *theory of mind* and *seeing the big picture* that were discussed in Part Two. Researchers refer to the ability to see the "big picture" as *central coherence*,[41] and it is an important factor in work performance. Central coherence allows us to shift focus between the big picture and the details, in order to accomplish a goal. People with autism may have weak central coherence, so they may be able to recall the exact details of something, yet miss the overall meaning; they typically think about things in the smallest possible parts.

Central coherence is related to *context*, the lens through which one views a situation or circumstance. It encompasses the ability to set priorities or learn from a previous situation that is like a current one. It also allows us to make sense of an idiom, such as "kick the report upstairs" or inexact language such as "get me a few numbers" by considering the context of the situation (i.e. the intent of the person speaking). Without understanding the context, an employee with autism may fail to see how an assignment relates to the bigger picture of a project, and his work may be incorrect, incomplete, or not relevant (see Figure 7.1).

Figure 7.1: Three components of work performance

Through *theory of mind* an employee interprets a work assignment by recognizing the goals his manager wants to achieve, and anticipating his manager's needs. In general, understanding the intentions of supervisors and colleagues helps an employee collaborate well with others, navigate workplace politics, and appreciate the perspectives of other members of his team. The difficulties with theory of mind that an employee on the spectrum may experience in social interactions may become evident in the workplace and result in his misinterpreting assignments or misreading a manager's intentions.

Work performance strengths

Individuals with autism can sustain their focus during long-lasting routine work, identify logical rules and patterns, process visual information, and remember vast amount of facts and information from highly specialized areas. They may show specific cognitive strengths such as *fluid intelligence*, which encompasses reasoning and novel problem-solving abilities that can have useful and creative applications in any workplace.[42, 43]

Typical work performance challenges

An employee on the autism spectrum with work performance challenges may:

- miss deadlines
- have difficulty with organization and setting priorities
- interpret instructions too literally
- need constant feedback
- act contrarian, stubborn, or refuse to change how he does something
- be easily frustrated.

Disclosure and accommodations for work performance issues

The profile of work performance issues for employees with autism will vary with the individual. While many will need accommodations to address issues with executive functioning, others may excel at organizing their work and managing their time; their work performance difficulties may be more related to issues with social interactions or the sensory challenges that will be discussed in Part Four.

The biggest advantage to disclosure for an employee on the autism spectrum and his manager is the understanding that challenges perceived as work performance issues are not related to the person's aptitude and ability to do the job. Instead, these issues may be a function of how the work is defined and delivered to that person. The accommodations for work performance issues include *understanding* how autism affects organizational skills in general, while *strategies* and *rules* involve clarifying instructions and structuring work clearly (see Table 7.2). A manager must ensure the individual understands the specifics of *what* he is supposed to do, as well as *how* and *when* to deliver it.

Table 7.2: Accommodations for work performance issues

	Definition	Example
Understanding	Ways of looking at work performance issues within the context of autism	People on the spectrum may have difficulty prioritizing because they think of every part of a task as equally important.
Strategies	Simple tactics that you can use	Create rules for certain tasks that should always be given priority, such as processing the weekly payroll.
Rules	Concrete statements that define parameters of acceptable behavior	"Always check with me first before you make any changes to this procedure."

In the next four chapters, *Organization, Time Management, Work Quality,* and *Emotional Regulation,* we will discuss the most typical work performance challenges for individuals on the autism spectrum and the various accommodations to help them work more efficiently and with less stress. The accommodations and management strategies discussed are not difficult, overly time-consuming, or costly. Many are good management practices that require some thought and effort, but are useful with all employees. Employees on the spectrum may take a bit more time to internalize the lessons from some of these strategies, but they will over time, resulting in less effort in making these accommodations in the future.

Chapter 8

ORGANIZATION

The need for *organizational skills* permeates every facet of the office environment, from managing time and deadlines to setting priorities and planning projects. In fact, the ability to organize the tasks of the day and set priorities is essential, not only for work but for life in general. In Part Two we stressed that *understanding* how individuals on the autism spectrum think and perceive the world was key to helping them manage social interactions. However, for issues relating to *organization* (and most work performance issues) understanding alone does little to solve the problem; they require coaching that addresses the specific skills necessary for performing at one's best.

Organization is like reverse-engineering: you start with a goal or task in mind, and then analyze its components. A person who is "disorganized" may not know how to start a task, break it into smaller parts, or prioritize the steps he needs to take. For example, the first task of the day for most employees is "getting to work on time," as shown in Figure 8.1.

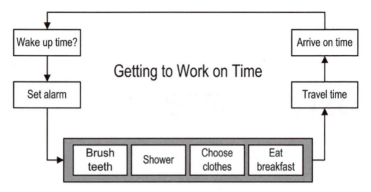

Figure 8.1: Getting to work on time

While this process may seem rather simple to most adults, it draws heavily on the *executive functioning skills* discussed in the introduction to Part Three. Getting to work on time (illustrated above) requires looking at the end goal (arriving at work at a specific time), then organizing the tasks involved into an efficient sequence, while factoring in the time it takes to get ready and travel to work, and how variations will affect the process (meeting at a client's office, going on a business trip, coming in earlier).

We rarely think about all that is involved in getting out the door in the morning, but to successfully start the work day, you must:

1. decide the night before what time you need to wake up the next morning

2. set an alarm clock to ensure you awake on time

3. decide on the activities and sequence of your morning routine—brush your teeth, shower, choose clothes appropriate for the day and dress, eat breakfast

4. prioritize these activities and allot an appropriate amount of time for each, so that you leave your house with enough time to get to your office or first activity.

For individuals on the spectrum, this "simple" process can be their first organizational challenge of the day. At work, they may also struggle with keeping track of schedules and due dates, planning and prioritizing tasks, and keeping the "big picture" in mind while focusing on details. In this chapter, we will cover the most common organizational issues in the workplace for employees with autism.

On a positive note:

- The ability of employees on the autism spectrum to remember and process minute details and detect patterns often results in creative solutions to complex problems.

- They excel at repetitive tasks that demand accuracy, rules, and routine and have a passion for researching and cataloging topics of interest. Their recall of information and willingness to share it often makes them a valuable resource among colleagues.

As you read this chapter, please remember that not all individuals with autism will display all the behaviors discussed. Each individual on the spectrum is different, and their challenges related to autism will be unique to them.

Section 8.1: He's so disorganized!

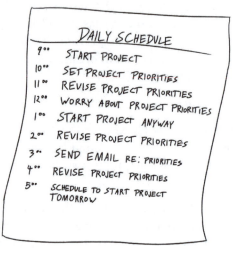

Topics covered

- Cannot plan work
- Cannot prioritize
- Cannot seem to get started
- Persistently late for work

Are you seeing these behaviors?

- You assign a task to an employee, but he can't keep track of the information he needs. *And you think to yourself, "He's so disorganized!"*

- When you give an employee a list of things you need him to do for the day, he does not complete them in the order of priority.

- An employee is late for work because he ran out of cereal and went to the store before work to buy more.

What are the underlying issues?
Organizational skills

The workplace often demands that you perform a wide range of tasks with varying levels of importance and different time frames. Being organized helps you structure your day, making you more efficient and less prone to distraction. Poor organizational skills are one of the hallmarks of executive function problems, because organizing tasks and projects involves many sub-skills. First, you must decide which aspects of the task you need to address. Next, you must distinguish the important factors of that task from the unimportant ones. Then, you must set a target date and start with the most important steps first, keeping in mind the other parts of the task that also need to be accomplished within a given amount of time.

Challenges with *organization* will vary with the individual. A colleague on the spectrum may be good at determining the steps involved in accomplishing a task, but may have difficulty determining which are the most important. Another colleague may be good at prioritizing, but not follow through on the less important aspects of a project. A researcher might be systematic and detailed when working on an area of interest, yet have difficulty producing organized paperwork or reports.

Conversation also requires *organization* and *prioritization*. When you interact with someone, your brain organizes the information you receive according to the relative importance of who is speaking and what they are telling you or asking you to do.

Organization helps us create and maintain systems to keep track of materials, information, and time. For example, documents are generally organized in folders according to hierarchies of related groups of information; each folder may contain other folders that hold different levels of detail. An effective filing system takes into account how the information will be used, and who will be using it. An employee with autism may have difficulty determining logical categories or may organize materials in a way that seems perfectly logical to him but is confusing to his colleagues.

Effective scheduling depends on planning and prioritizing tasks so they can be accomplished within a specific time frame. Most employees know how to use day planners, scheduling software, and electronic calendars, but an individual with autism may need help setting up a scheduling system and developing a routine for adding items or dividing a task into multiple days.

> *"One of the tools I use to keep myself organized, keep appointments and keep my whole life from personal to professional organized is my iPad. I use the calendar function and have it synched with Google, so I get reminders regularly and can see if somebody wants to schedule something with me."*

An employee on the spectrum may have difficulty arranging his day so that tasks with a high priority are completed before others. Going over the schedule at the start of the day with a manager or a colleague who understands the department will help an employee learn which types of tasks should come first, as well as how much time should be allotted.

Planning

Every facet of the workplace involves planning, from daily schedules to projects and timelines, as well as adjustments to them. The executive functions of *planning* and *prioritizing* are core organizational skills in the workplace; they involve making decisions about where to direct attention and what steps to take, as well as their order of importance. Planning a project involves keeping the goal, or "big picture," in mind, while breaking down the tasks into more manageable parts.

Time management (covered in Chapter 9) is an important aspect of planning, as you need to know not only *when* the work is due, but also *how much time* you should put aside to complete it. Telling an employee with autism to "make time" in his schedule or to "set aside some time" when assigning work is not sufficient, because he may not be sure *where* in his schedule he should carve out the hours, or be aware of how working on this task might impact deadlines for other work.

When planning a project, an individual on the spectrum may not consider all of the resources he will need, or how he will get them. For example, creating a report or presentation is not always a straightforward process. Does the receiving audience expect it in a specific format? If so, who do you contact to get a template or sample? If there is no dictated format, who should you contact to confirm how the report should look and what it should contain? What other information besides the data will you need, and who do you contact to get it?

Setting priorities

Planning efficiently depends on the ability to *set priorities* for investing time and effort. The demands of the workplace are constantly shifting, so employees need to be able to prioritize what is important and complete that work first. No doubt you have heard of the "80/20 Rule": 20% of your activities will account for 80% of your success. Determining which tasks fall into the "20%" category involves stepping back and seeing the work that you need to do within the context of your department's goals, as well as the time and resources available.

Individuals on the spectrum typically focus on details at the expense of the "big picture," as we will discuss in Section 8.2. Consequently, an employee might be good at analyzing a project and laying out the details of what needs to be done, but have difficulty pinpointing those steps that are the most critical, because he views each one as equally important. He also might not recognize that the order in which he completes those parts might affect other aspects of a project, especially if the work will be used by others. On the other hand, an employee might set the proper priorities, but fail to follow up on the less important items or have trouble maintaining attention to the more mundane aspects of the project.

When given a list of tasks to complete, an employee may not be aware of their relative importance, and instead work through the list in sequence.

"I would write a list out of what my tasks were for the day and for the week. And then I would prioritize those tasks and ask my manager, 'Is this top priority?'...otherwise I'd just go in the order I received them, regardless of what the issue was."

Explaining to an employee on the spectrum why a task or procedure is important will help him learn to prioritize and stay on track. However, individuals with autism tend to adhere to rules rigidly, and may resist adjusting because a priority has changed. They may be confused when asked to do a less important task first to get it out of the way, when there is not enough time to tackle one with a higher priority.

When working on setting priorities with an employee on the spectrum, you can provide him with a series of "mini-decisions" to determine if one thing is more important than another:

- *Dependencies*: Does a task depend on the completion of other tasks?

- *Time*: Is one task due sooner than another or has someone asked for something to be done immediately?

- *Person*: Who requested the task?

If people assigning tasks are at different levels within the organization, the manager should determine whose request the employee will satisfy first.

Getting started

To create a plan and prioritize, however, you need to "get started," which is managed by the executive function of *task initiation*. Although we sometimes delay tackling certain activities that we do not particularly want to do, for most of us knowing *how* to start a task is largely intuitive. For example, during tax season many people begin by simply collecting all of their income statements and expense receipts as the first step to categorizing them. An individual on the spectrum, however, might quickly become overwhelmed because he feels the need to first create extensive lists of expense categories or understand the nuances of the current tax law, bypassing a rather obvious and easily completed first step.

Organization and planning involves knowing how to adjust when something does not go as planned. If an individual with autism is persistently late for work, it may be related to a break in the chain of events that he must go through, such as getting up or walking out the door. The employee may also have difficulty starting the process or continuing it when an adjustment needs to be made along the way. Unexpected deviations such as running out of cereal, weather changes, and transit interruptions may make it difficult to move past that part of his routine, because he is unsure of how to work around it.

People on the spectrum are generally very persistent, and will follow through on tasks when they are clear about goals, sequence of steps, and resources needed.

What can you do about an employee who is not organized?

It is helpful to keep in mind that most people on the spectrum function more effectively within structure, but they are not always good at creating the structure themselves. In general:

- Written lists remove the guesswork about what to do next, and they are an effective way to keep track of ongoing tasks, especially for individuals who may have difficulty remembering multiple verbal requests.

- If necessary, assign a colleague who is familiar with the department to help an employee with autism develop daily and weekly To Do lists to keep him on track.

- An employee can check in with his manager for a few minutes at the beginning of the day to prioritize his schedule or carve out time for a last-minute task or a project that spans multiple days.

If an individual is persistently late for work, he might need help creating a plan for his morning routine that factors in things that affect the chain of steps, such as inclement weather or an alternate bus route.

Planning a project involves breaking it down into smaller tasks, so provide samples or completed examples whenever possible. Working *backward* from the completed task or goal, have the employee compile a list of steps needed to complete the project, then review it with him to ensure all the steps are within scope. Help him prioritize the steps and create sub-tasks for each (see Figure 8.2).

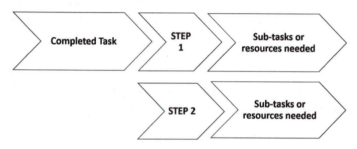

Figure 8.2: Working backward to plan a project

Another way to help the employee prioritize is by *dependency*, *time*, or *person*:

- If a task *depends on* additional information, resources, or another task's completion, do that task first.

- If there are no dependencies, look at the *time frame* to determine if one task is due immediately or sooner than the other tasks.

- If *multiple people* are asking the individual for work, designate whose request should be satisfied first.

You can also help an employee learn how to set priorities by asking him to create pairs of tasks and put a checkmark next to the one with the higher priority, or create rules for certain tasks that should always be given priority, such as processing the weekly payroll.

When assigning a task, always check for understanding. Rather than just asking the employee what he is going to do first, ask *what is most important, what information* he may need, and in *what order* he is going to proceed.

If an employee has difficulty with initiation, he may not know how to start or what to start on first, so you may need to make a direct suggestion such as, "Why don't you start with XYZ first?" Detailed lists that have been prioritized beforehand will help an employee keep track of the next task in the sequence; however, if he needs a jumpstart, suggest starting with a task that is a lower priority but is easier to do.

Related material

- Section 8.2

- Chapter 9: Time Management

Section 8.2: Just give me the main points!

319 Conifers at 100% Precipitation During the Winter Solstice

Topics covered

- Misses the "big picture"
- Provides too much detail
- Cannot give a simple or direct explanation

Are you seeing these behaviors?

- You have asked members of your team to email you a short update on the status of a project. One person sends you a seven-page memo. *And you think to yourself, "Just give me the main points!"*

- You've asked a colleague for an update on a project, but when you ask him to clarify a point, he launches into an overly detailed explanation.

- When asked a question, an employee gives you his entire thought process.

What are the underlying issues?

The "big picture"

As discussed in Part Two, the neurological makeup of individuals on the spectrum results in ways of thinking that are fundamentally different from that of *neuro-typicals*, such as *theory of mind*—the ability to consider another person's perspective. A person's *cognitive style* reflects his preferred way of thinking, remembering, and solving problems, such as extracting the "big picture" from a mass of details. This is an effective way of processing information, as it allows us to spontaneously get the gist of something without needing all the specifics (i.e. "seeing the forest instead of the trees"). We then work from the "top down," filling in details when necessary to fit the larger mental picture.

In the business world, people who excel at big picture thinking and envisioning broad goals are referred to as "strategic thinkers" or "visionaries," while "tactical thinkers" excel at implementing the details that make the plan work. Most of us, however, have aspects of each type of thinking and can switch between them as needed.

In the workplace, seeing the *big picture* provides an efficient way of organizing our perceptions and experiences, so that we can then plan and prioritize. It allows us to integrate multiple sources of information from current data and prior knowledge, while factoring in relevant aspects of the situation (see Figure 8.3).

To successfully plan and complete a project, we first need to get the big picture of the goal, and then keep it in mind while organizing and prioritizing all the relevant aspects of the tasks involved. Once the roadmap has been developed, we then focus on the details to get the job done.

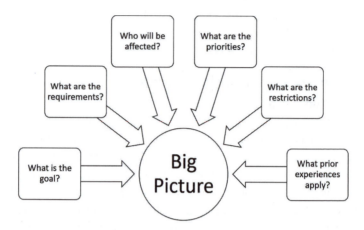

Figure 8.3: Components of the "big picture" at work

Focusing on details

An individual on the autism spectrum generally tends to focus mainly on the details, and has difficulty "connecting the dots" (i.e. processing facts and bits of information within context). For example, he can recite the names of every character and recount all of the dialogue in a movie, but may not be able to give a summary of the plot. *Central coherence* is the cognitive style that refers to our ability to pull information from multiple sources into a unified whole, and researchers suggest that this is a key area of weakness for people on the autism spectrum.[44]

Central coherence allows us spontaneously to focus both on details as well as the whole. In Chapter 6 we discussed how seeing the "big picture" aids in facial recognition, when we associate the components of a face with a mental image of a specific person, and how we create a unified impression of what a person is thinking and feeling from the integration of facial expression, tone of voice, body language, and words spoken. Understanding the "big picture" makes it possible to detect sarcasm, as well as apply a social rule from one situation to others that are similar.

"Being on the spectrum you just love to focus on every little detail there is."

People on the spectrum *can* see the whole, but it might take them longer because of their tendency to process details from the "bottom up," fitting each piece together until a pattern emerges. To illustrate, most of us build a puzzle by first referring to the picture on the box (the *context* of what we are building), then assembling the frame, because those pieces are generally the easiest to recognize. Someone on the spectrum, however, may not need to depend on the context of the picture to complete the puzzle. Instead, he will analyze the pieces to see how they relate to each other: how piece A fits into piece B, then how A and B together fit into piece C, and so on. As he builds out the elements of the picture, eventually the concept will emerge. This type of thinking works well when analyzing processes, procedures, and computer code that have interrelated elements.

An individual on the spectrum might have difficulty focusing on both the overall idea and the small details at the same time, which may affect his ability to plan and prioritize. When working on a project or solving a problem, he may also become overwhelmed when trying to process information from more than one source at a time; this can result in taking an overly narrow focus that may overlook obvious factors or concerns. When working in a team, he may fully understand his individual role, but struggle to understand how he fits into the team's wider agenda.

Individuals on the spectrum tend to think from the "bottom up," relying on their exceptional ability to see patterns and find connections in facts and details, which eventually leads to a "bird's-eye view" of whatever they are studying. To them, every detail is integral to the whole, and their ability to relate multidisciplinary facts and ideas can lead to creative and meaningful insights. According to world-renowned autism spokesperson Temple Grandin, "When I solve the problem, it is not top-down and theory driven. Instead, I look at how all the little pieces fit together to form a bigger picture."[45]

Unlike most people, individuals on the spectrum need not rely on a framework or context to process details, so they are less apt to be swayed by convention and assumptions, which makes them excellent proofreaders, error-checkers, and problem-solvers. They may also excel in data analysis, and working with technology, procedures, and programming.

> *"I think one of the great skills we possess is the ability to observe things in a way that says, 'That's really smart, that's great technology, this works fantastic,' or 'That's really flawed—there are ten things you can remove from there and still be just as effective without wasting so much time.'"*

Over time an employee *can* learn to broaden his scope, although a manager or colleague might need to provide *context*, such as "This is important *because…*," or a cue, such as "As you analyze the figures for this quarter, *remember to account for XYZ*." Keep in mind that attention to detail and the ability to perceive what others may have missed are valuable assets in many fields of work!

Providing too much detail

In the workplace, succinct communication is critical, whether it is summarizing a meeting, explaining a process or answering an email. A common complaint about employees on the spectrum is that they provide "too much detail," resulting in emails or summaries that go on for pages, overly detailed explanations, and rambling answers to simple questions. While these behaviors all relate to missing the "big picture," there are differences in how to address them.

> *"'Terse' was the word in one review, 'You have to be terse.'"*

Summarizing, or extracting the main points, is managed by the executive function of *prioritizing*, which we discussed in the previous section. It depends on our ability to differentiate the details that are relevant from those that are not, as well as a *sense of time* (e.g. how much time someone can spare to read an email or listen to a presentation). However, a colleague on the spectrum may feel *every* detail is important and be reluctant to leave some out, or may omit key points when asked to condense.

For example, at a staff meeting where each person has two minutes to provide an update on the project, a colleague spends ten minutes. After the meeting, he is told that in the future he should spend no more than two minutes and include five bullet points. At the next meeting, he speaks for the two minutes, but leaves out all the salient information. A more effective strategy involves working with the employee one-on-one to help him figure out the most important information that he needs to convey and how to present it in the allotted time.

The cognitive world of individuals on the autism spectrum is made up of interconnected facts and details that are part of more complex mental models. This makes it challenging for an employee with autism to provide a simple or direct explanation, because in his mind there may be many contingencies; skipping the details is equivalent to ignoring part of the solution. If he works in a technical field, understanding what level of detail is appropriate or what degree of accuracy is sufficient can also be a problem.

"I was always very conscious of all of the technical details. Whenever that happened, they would just tell me, 'slow down' or 'stop already'."

This may be due, in part, to theory of mind—not looking at things from the listener or recipient's point of view and considering how much information they need. Being clear about the length of explanation and level of detail you expect will help a colleague with autism stay within those parameters. Similarly, it may be difficult for the employee to give a definitive answer without a lot of qualification, so explain what type of answer you will need, and give him the opportunity to express any concerns in writing.

When neuro-typicals are asked a question, they often start with a general answer, and then justify their response by providing details. Prioritizing and summarizing information into a general answer may be difficult for an individual on the spectrum to do quickly, since he may need to process the pertinent details *first*, before he can formulate an answer. For example, when you ask an employee, "Do you think you can get this done by the end of the day?" he might think out loud, going through his entire schedule as he tries to process the question, so you might need to give him some leeway while he gets to the answer.

How do you deal with an employee who misses the "big picture"?

Perhaps the most effective accommodation is to understand that while neuro-typicals intuitively "connect the dots," or recognize the context, employees with autism may not. However, keep in mind that while individuals on the spectrum may *prefer* to focus on details, they can learn to be aware of the "big picture" if they are given some guidance, although it may take bit longer and they may need to be reminded. Providing the parameters of a project, such as a list of the goals, requirements, and restrictions will help shape the work requested along those lines.

Whenever possible, provide the context such as:

- "This is important because…"

- "I'm going to need to know yes or no."

- "Your analysis needs to take into account last year as well as this year."

It may be difficult for an employee on the spectrum to limit the amount of information he provides. However, merely stating "That was too much information; give me less" will most likely result in the employee replying, "I can't—everything's important." You need to sit down with him and explain which pieces of information you thought were important and why. When summarizing a written document, highlighting the most important points in one color and those that are secondary in another color will provide the employee with a visual cue for which information should be addressed first.

Whenever possible, provide the context of *time* (e.g. how much time someone can spare to read an email or listen to a presentation). If an employee provides too much detail when giving oral presentations, give him a time limit. Work with him to keep the "big picture" in mind while prioritizing the key elements, so he can narrow down the amount of information or level of detail to fit the amount of time allotted. An employee may become anxious about omitting material that he considers relevant; always acknowledge his concern, then suggest that he document it in writing.

If a team member on the spectrum is responsible for meeting minutes or a report, show him an example of how much information he should include, then ask him to create a list of points that he feels are most important. Go through the list together and explain *which* information can be eliminated and *why*.

Rules about the length and format of emails will help an employee be more concise, such as "When you send me an update on the project, give me the five most important points as bullets." To help the individual deliver information during updates and meetings, use cues, such as:

- "Give me the three most important points."
- "What can you tell me in five minutes?"
- "Give me a condensed version."
- "What's the most important next step I need to take?"

It may be challenging for an individual with autism to give a quick response that involves an evaluation or a decision, since he may need to first go through the relevant details before he can formulate an answer. If the question is not complex, he may need to think it through "out loud," so just give him some time. However, if it requires more thought in terms of priorities or procedures, ask the employee to send you his answer in writing or to come back to you within a specified time period once he has had time to formulate his answer.

The detail-oriented thinking of an employee on the spectrum can benefit a team, but he may need an explanation as to how his individual work coordinates with the rest of the team members. Assign a team member to check in with him to make sure his work is on target and stays focused on those details that are relevant.

Whenever possible, look for opportunities that will allow an individual with autism to use his ability to focus on details and think tactically in favor of tasks that require a more strategic "big picture" perspective.

Related material

- Chapter 6: Social Interaction

Organization: Accommodations summary

Executive functioning is a term for the cognitive processes that help us manage and control our thoughts and actions. Executive functioning skills are not directly related to IQ, but rather to how well we use the intelligence that we have. Our ability to organize, plan, prioritize, initiate, and transition between tasks and activities depends on our executive functioning capabilities.

Organization is like reverse-engineering; you start with a goal or task in mind, and then analyze its components. A person who is "disorganized" or seems to struggle with time management may not know how to start a task, break it into smaller parts, or prioritize the steps he needs to take. Challenges with organization will vary with the individual. A colleague on the spectrum may be good at determining the steps involved in accomplishing a task, but may have difficulty determining which are the most important. Another colleague may be good at prioritizing, but not follow through on the less important aspects of a project.

The executive functions of *planning* and *prioritizing* are core organizational skills in the workplace as they involve making decisions about where to direct attention and what steps to take, in addition to their order of importance. Planning a project involves keeping the goal, or "big picture," in mind, while breaking down the tasks into more manageable parts.

The cognitive world of individuals on the autism spectrum is made up of interconnected facts and details that are part of more complex mental models. This makes it challenging for an employee with autism to provide a simple or direct explanation, because in his mind there may be many contingencies; skipping the details is equivalent to ignoring part of the solution. But people on the spectrum are generally very persistent, and will follow through on tasks when they are clear about goals, sequence of steps, and resources needed.

Due to their executive functioning challenges in the area of organization, employees on the spectrum may exhibit difficulties in the following areas:

- planning

- prioritizing

- initiating

- seeing the "big picture"

- providing too much detail.

Individuals with autism process and organize information differently than neuro-typical individuals. What seems like a logical progression of tasks to most people may not appear so to someone on the spectrum. This differing perspective can allow individuals on the autism spectrum to take new and creative approaches to problem-solving.

Because employees on the spectrum organize information differently, they may need a different approach to the process of planning and prioritizing their work:

- Go over the schedule at the start of the day with the employee, emphasizing which types of tasks should come first, as well as how much time should be allotted.

- Assign a colleague who is familiar with the department to help him develop daily and weekly To Do lists to keep him on track.

- Working backward from the completed task or goal, have the employee compile a list of steps needed to complete the project, then review it with him to ensure all the steps are within scope.

- Provide samples or completed examples of the expected work product whenever possible.

- If an individual is persistently late for work, create a plan for his morning routine that factors in things that affect the chain of steps, such as inclement weather or an alternate bus route.

Prioritizing:

- Explain why a task or procedure is important to help the employee learn to prioritize and stay on track.

- Provide him with a series of "mini-decisions" to determine if one thing is more important than another.

- If people assigning tasks are at different levels within the organization, the manager should determine whose request the employee will satisfy first.

- Check in with the employee for a few minutes at the beginning of each day to prioritize his schedule, carve out time for a last-minute task, or timetable a project that spans multiple days.

- When assigning a task, always check for understanding. Rather than just asking the employee what he is going to do first, ask *what is most important, what information* he may need, and in *what order* he is going to proceed.

Initiating:

- Make a direct suggestion such as "Why don't you start with XYZ first?"

- Provide detailed lists that have been prioritized beforehand.

- Suggest starting with a task that is a lower priority but is easier to do.

Individuals on the autism spectrum generally tend to focus on the details and can have difficulty seeing the "big picture." Providing structure and context helps them integrate their work into the broader project:

- Provide the parameters of a project, such as a list of the goals, requirements, and restrictions to help shape the work requested along those lines.

- Give an explanation as to how his individual work coordinates with other team members.

- Assign a team member to check in and make sure his work is on target and that he stays focused on those details that are relevant.

- Look for opportunities that will allow him to use his ability to focus on details and think tactically in favor of tasks that require a more strategic "big picture" perspective.

Too much detail:

- Sit down with the employee and explain which pieces of information you thought were important and why.

- Show him an example of how much information he should include for work that is repetitive (e.g. meeting notes).

- Highlight the most important points of the information in one color and those that are secondary in another color to provide the employee with a visual cue for which issues should be addressed first.

- Provide the context of *time* (e.g. how much time someone can spare to read an email or listen to a presentation).

- Provide rules about the length and format of emails and presentations.

- Always acknowledge his concern, then suggest that he document it in writing, if an employee becomes anxious about omitting material that he considers relevant.

Chapter 9

TIME MANAGEMENT

Time is a concept that we intuitively grasp, but how we perceive time is relative; most of us think of a second as a short span of time, but to an Olympic speed skater, shaving a second off his race time is huge.

Time management is an *executive function* issue, because it involves how you organize your time and understand the passage of time. No doubt you have noticed that time can slip away when you are absorbed in a task, or that it grinds to a halt when you are bored or uninterested. Additionally, how you manage your time depends on whether you need to accomplish many tasks in a short period, or work on one task for an extended time. Individuals with autism often have a poor ability to estimate the amount of time needed to complete a project and may not notice how much time has elapsed when working on a task.

Many time management issues are interrelated with other executive functions, such as the ability to shift gears and transition to another task, knowing how to begin a task and when to stop, and the ability to monitor and evaluate one's own performance. Other cognitive factors that affect time management are the awareness of time, the ability to focus, and processing speed, as shown in Figure 9.1.

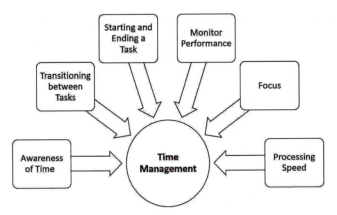

Figure 9.1: Time management factors

Technology, such as digital calendars, smartphone timers, and email reminders can improve time management; but for individuals on the autism spectrum, knowing how to manage their time at work may be a challenge. In this chapter, we will cover the most common time management issues in the workplace, including awareness of time, transitioning between tasks, focus, and multitasking.

On a positive note:

- Many individuals with autism can focus on a task for long periods of time without becoming distracted. They have a strong work ethic, with a commitment to quality and accuracy.

- The techniques for addressing many time management challenges for individuals on the spectrum can benefit all employees and improve productivity.

As you read this chapter, please remember that not all individuals with autism will display all the behaviors discussed. Each individual on the spectrum is different, and their challenges related to autism will be unique to them.

Section 9.1: He never gets it done on time!

Topics covered

- Loses track of time
- Procrastinates and frequently misses deadlines
- Takes forever to do a simple task
- Learns at a different pace than others
- Cannot shift gears quickly

Are you seeing these behaviors?

- Whenever you assign a report to an employee, he always asks for an extension. *And you think to yourself, "He never gets it done on time!"*

- At team updates, one employee is always behind in his project work.

- An employee becomes annoyed when a meeting does not start at the exact time it was scheduled.

What are the underlying issues?

Awareness of time

The demands of the workplace are constantly changing. Effective time management involves accurately estimating how much time a task will take, deciding how to divide your time throughout the day, and how to meet deadlines. While the electronic organizers on smartphones and computers help in keeping track of appointments and scheduling tasks, it is up to each employee to decide *how* to fill his schedule. Some people on the autism spectrum are very organized and have no trouble meeting deadlines, while others may have difficulties with scheduling, because they do not have an inner clock that allows them to accurately sense the passage of time. For example, when asked to do something in an hour, they may not know how quickly they need to work, or whether that time frame is reasonable.

Some deadlines are set in stone, others are approximate. Meetings may start on time or be delayed. The workday might end at 5 P.M. for most employees, yet last much later for managers who are up against a deadline. People on the autism spectrum generally consider time absolute; they tend to be punctual, assuming a meeting will begin at the *exact* time and may become anxious when it does not. Similarly, they may expect to leave at the usual quitting time, when the rest of the team feels the need to stay later to complete a time-critical task.

The *context of time* is an important factor in planning, because the time a task requires must fit into the amount of time available. When assigning a task to an employee on the spectrum, being specific about deadlines and time frames, such as "by three o'clock Thursday afternoon" will be less confusing than "by the end of the week." Providing the employee with an estimate of how much time he should set aside, as well as the priority of the task, will help him know how to fit it into his schedule.

Procrastination

We all tend to put off the things that we do not want to do. Employees with autism generally have a great work ethic and are eager to do a job well, yet may frequently miss deadlines. What might look like procrastination might be due to not knowing how or where to start, such as the issues with the executive functions of *task initiation*, *planning*, and *prioritization* discussed in the previous chapter. Workplace distractions may also be a factor; individuals on the spectrum do not have a "pause button," and if they are interrupted may need to go back to the beginning of a task.

On the other hand, some individuals on the spectrum may be so anxious to complete work assigned at the beginning of the week, that they speed through it and work late until it's completed, then have nothing to do for the rest of the week.

> *"Because I have very poor time management skills, instead of procrastinating on things, like some people would do, I try to get everything done as quickly as possible."*

"Simple" tasks

Another aspect of time management is determining how thoroughly you can do a task, given the amount of time you have; the scope and depth of an assignment will vary with the time frame. For example, a project update for a team meeting that is due in a few hours will contain less information than a formal written report that is due in a few weeks. Most employees on the spectrum want their work to be at a high level of quality, and they might put more time and effort into a task than is necessary. Because of their perfectionism and attention to detail, they may take an excessive amount of time to complete tasks, even "simple" ones. This is often related to an employee not understanding the *context* of the request. If a task should take no longer than an hour, specify what the work should encompass (*scope*) and the level of detail (*depth*) you expect, given the time frame.

Keep in mind that a task that seems "simple" to you, may not be to an individual with autism. Any task encompasses *input* (the request itself), *processing* (how the request was interpreted), and *output* (the format and content of the work delivered), and if the employee is not clear about any of these, he may get "stuck."

Processing speed and learning

Processing speed is not an executive function *per se* or related to intelligence, although processing speed does affect a person's ability to sort through information quickly, such as keeping up with the back and forth flow of conversations. It is an important factor in effective time management, because regulating your processing speed allows you to control how slowly or quickly you perform a task based upon its relative importance and time frame. Processing speed can be affected by various factors— we have all experienced the feeling of being in cognitive "slow motion" when emotionally distressed, or the mad dash that ensues when you have put something off until the last minute.

Employees on the spectrum with slow processing speed may appear to be focused, but not get much done. Factors that may hamper their ability to process information include being overwhelmed by too much information at once, needing more time to make decisions or give answers, and having trouble executing instructions when multiple requests are made at the same time. On the other hand, processing speed is affected by one's knowledge base and experience, and some employees with autism may be able to process certain types of *nonverbal* information, such as computer code, diagrams, and technical data more quickly than their colleagues.

Individuals on the spectrum may be perceived as unmotivated or lazy when they take longer to initiate or complete simple tasks, or respond to a request. As discussed previously, we use our executive functions to create a mental roadmap that serves as a guide for what to do first, next, and so on to complete a task. Executive functioning depends on processing speed to work efficiently, so a colleague with autism who is slow to process information may not be able to organize materials and thoughts, set priorities, or get started in a timely manner. For example, an account manager assigned to summarize and circulate the minutes of the meeting may take more time than expected because he is "stuck" deciding what to include in the summary and who should receive it.

> *"I had issues with time management because I have my own style of working, and in particular, my own learning curve which is slow at the beginning, but then rises very quickly."*

How you process information also affects how quickly you learn. Individuals on the spectrum learn through direct experience, and may have to do something repeatedly before it makes sense. They tend to be visual thinkers, and often absorb something new by analyzing the details or individual parts that interest them the most and seeing how they fit together. It might take time to integrate those details into a global concept that they can visualize and implement, but once they figure it out, their understanding will be at a high level and they will be able to work very efficiently, because they have already integrated many different contingencies, relationships, and exceptions.

Transitioning

Throughout the workday, we constantly "shift gears" as we move between tasks, engage in conversations, begin a meeting or manage interruptions. The executive function of *transitioning* involves switching one's focus of attention or "shifting" quickly from one thought or task to another, such as writing a report after working on another (possibly unrelated) task. People on the autism spectrum can have trouble with transitioning and getting "stuck in a gear," because they are very deeply involved in what they are currently doing. They may have an intense form of attention, called *hyperfocus* (covered in Section 9.2), and may need extra time to pull their focus away from the task at hand and refocus it on something different.

For example, a manager assigns three tasks for the day to an employee on the spectrum, with the expectation that each task will take about two hours—a total of six hours. However, at the end of six hours, the work is still not completed. Although the employee can complete each task within the allotted two hours, he might need time *in between* tasks to transition from one mental set to another, especially if the tasks are not related. An individual that has issues with transitioning will often insist on extending a discussion after the subject has changed, because he is not able to move quickly from one topic to the next.

Disengaging from one activity, changing gears, and focusing on another activity requires large amounts of energy and effort. Give an employee on the spectrum a break between tasks so he can fully extract himself from one task before starting on another. Sometimes physical movement, such as a quick walk down the hall, can help the employee make a mental break from a completed task, so he can start on the next one.

When deadlines are not met, analyzing the symptoms of difficulties with time management and getting feedback from the employee as to what might be the problem is key to finding a solution. Ask specific questions, such as "Once you completed this task, how long did it take you to get started on the next one?" or "Are there specific times of day or types of tasks when shifting gears is the most challenging for you?"

> *"If the building was burning down, and somebody told me to process payroll, I'm going to process payroll before I leave the building, because that's the next thing on my list."*

Another type of transitioning in the workplace involves accepting a deviation from what was expected and having the *flexibility* to adapt one's plans when necessary. Routines and predictability provide structure and security for individuals with autism, so they may have transitioning issues associated with changes in routine or environment, such as planned activities that are canceled or rescheduled, or organizational, procedural, or location changes. An employee may also become overwhelmed when multiple people assign tasks, because he might assume that everything needs to be worked on simultaneously, or he is uncertain of how to deal with conflicting priorities.

How do you deal with an employee who never gets it done on time?

Strategies for addressing time management are not limited to individuals on the autism spectrum; the field of *coaching* was initially developed in the corporate setting to help people work more effectively by addressing some of the executive function issues discussed in this section.

Many of the suggested accommodations regarding time management will require a manager or colleague to be more specific when assigning tasks. Although this may seem like extra work, eventually this type of communication becomes second nature and benefits *all* employees.

When you assign a task or project to an employee with autism, putting it in the *context of time* will help him know how much time the task requires and how the work will fit into the time that he has available. To avoid misinterpretation or confusion, any time-based request should be concrete and specific, with exact deadlines or time frames; an indication of the scope and depth expected, given the allotted time; and the level of priority (see Table 9.1):

Table 9.1: Specific time-based requests

	Vague	Specific
Deadlines	"I need the report by the middle of the week."	"Give me the completed report by 5 P.M. on Wednesday."
Time frames	"It shouldn't take you too long."	"Do not spend more than an hour on it."
Scope and depth	"Give a progress report at tomorrow's meeting."	"Your progress report to the team should be two minutes or less, and it should include short updates on X, Y, and Z."
Priority	"This isn't due until next month."	"You do not need to focus on this now, but I want you start on it in two weeks, so you will be able to complete it by the 30th."

Email and smartphones are easy ways to help an employee on the spectrum manage time. For example, a team leader can help the employee keep up with team assignments with email reminders. If the employee loses track of time because he is absorbed in a task, he can use timers and alarms on a smartphone or computer to remind him it is time to finish the task at hand and start another assignment.

Whenever possible, allow an employee on the spectrum to complete one task before he moves to another. However, if he needs to return to a task, he can use "sticky notes" (either paper or on the computer) to mark his place and remind himself of what he needs to do next.

If an employee has difficulty with transitioning, go through the day's schedule so he will be mentally prepared. When the work includes shifting gears, an individual may need a 15- or 30-minute warning, such as "In 30 minutes you need to wrap up and move on to the next task on your schedule." In general, try not to assign a task "on the fly," but if you do need an employee with autism to work on something else, give him some time to extract himself from what he was doing. Keep in mind that the individual may become anxious about getting his other work for the day completed and may need help adjusting his schedule to accommodate the change.

To help an individual on the spectrum handle transitions:

- Schedule at least 15 minutes in between appointments or activities to give him the chance to put closure on what he has been doing and mentally prepare for the next task.

- Have the employee set a timer so he will know when to move to another task.

- Physical movement or a change in environment can help an individual get out of hyperfocus. Have the employee stand up when he is at the end of a task or the timer goes off. If necessary, he can take a short walk to mentally let go of the previous task and move to the next one.

- If an employee is on several teams or reports to multiple people, have his work assignments come through one person (a manager or colleague) who can coordinate them.

Managers and colleagues can help employees with other time management issues in various ways:

- Create a To Do list with large tasks divided into smaller tasks and enter the estimated time needed for each task.

- Maintain a wall calendar with color-coded due dates and tasks for each project.

- Practice together how to "guesstimate" the time needed for a task or sequences of tasks to help in setting a reasonable work pace.

- Schedule regular meetings to discuss the progress of long-term projects and determine whether existing deadlines are still feasible.

- Set up guidelines to limit the amount of time spent during unstructured breaks.

Related material

- Section 9.2

- Chapter 8: Organization

Section 9.2: I need him to multitask!

Topics covered

- Focuses intently on one thing
- Cannot multitask
- Complains about interruptions

Are you seeing these behaviors?

- You ask an employee to assist you on a time-sensitive project, and he tells you he cannot because he is already working on the small task you assigned him that morning. *And you think to yourself, "I need him to multitask!"*

- During a weekly meeting with a team member, you realize he is only working on one of the three tasks you assigned.

- When you briefly interrupt a colleague to ask a question, he stares at you blankly.

What's the underlying issue?
Hyperfocus

"My ability to stay focused is unlimited."

Hyperfocus is a style of thinking that is very deep, concentrated, and pleasurable to the person doing it. When in a career-related area, hyperfocus often translates into excellent problem-solving skills and subject-matter expertise—both highly valued in the workplace. Countless scientists, writers, and artists on the autism spectrum have made significant contributions to their fields in large part because of their ability to stay focused.

> *"Put somebody with Asperger's in a room and say, 'OK, here's the problem, I need an answer—work on it,' and I guarantee you that person is going to come up with an answer."*

Many individuals with autism consider themselves "information junkies" because of their intense interest in a narrow area and their ability to research, absorb, and retrieve vast amounts of highly detailed or technical information. However, while hyperfocus can be a strength, it often presents challenges when an employee needs to transition quickly between tasks, change routines, or multitask.

Individuals with autism tend to become absorbed in tasks that they find stimulating and rewarding; in fact, most people can become "lost" in an activity where they feel enjoyment, concentration, and deep involvement. Psychologist and researcher Mihaly Csikszentmihalyi calls this state of optimal experience *flow*—when people engaged in an activity chosen for its own sake concentrate so fully, they forget about time and the world around them.[46]

Although these two mental states are in many ways similar, hyperfocus may cause an employee to become so immersed in a task that he becomes oblivious to everything else going on around him, resulting in time management issues and problems completing other assigned tasks. Because of their preference for detail-oriented thinking, individuals on the spectrum may spend more time than is warranted intensely pursuing detailed information that is not relevant to the task.

You can help an employee productively use his ability to hyperfocus by assigning tasks that are in his area of expertise. Depending on the individual, he may prefer to alternate them with other tasks or group them together, so he can work uninterrupted for a longer period.

"Having the ability to create your own schedule around the things that you do well...really helps you manage your time."

Multitasking

When you have multiple tasks to accomplish, you need to organize your time so you can complete the tasks within a specific time frame without forgetting any of them. *Multitasking* implies doing many tasks simultaneously, but the brain cannot effectively focus on more than one thing at the same time (reflected in the recent "texting while driving" laws). Multitasking is actually *serial* tasking—shifting from one task to another in rapid succession. Rather than completing one task at a time, you focus your attention for a shorter period on a *task segment*, switch to a segment for a different task, then return to the next segment of the first task. This results in many more transitions than just doing one task at a time (see Figure 9.2).

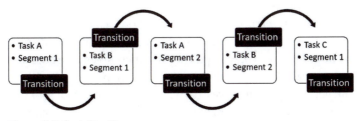

Figure 9.2: Serial tasking

Many workplaces assume that employees who multitask are more productive, but switching back and forth through tasks forces the brain to shift focus and rapidly turn rules on and off, which drains one's energy and can impact overall performance. Researchers at Stanford University studied frequent multitaskers who felt switching between multiple tasks boosted their performance and found that they performed worse than people who liked to do one thing at a time. The multitaskers were slower at switching from one task to another and had more trouble organizing their thoughts and filtering out irrelevant information.[47]

As discussed in Section 9.1, individuals on the autism spectrum can have challenges with *transitioning*, because they may be so absorbed in one task that it takes great cognitive effort to pull themselves out of it and turn their attention to something else. If asked to multitask, they will be subject to many more transitions than if allowed to finish one task before working on another, which may make them less productive because of the time needed to switch focus.

> *"It is very difficult for me to let go of something and move to something else, because I'm still thinking about it."*

Individuals on the spectrum can excel at accuracy and quality and are most productive when they can complete one task, no matter how small, before moving to the next. Helping the employee group "simultaneous" tasks into a *series* of smaller related *sequential tasks* may reduce problems with transitioning and the tendency to hyperfocus.

Interruptions

Workplace interruptions, such as phone calls, emails, and impromptu conversations, also involve transitioning and serial tasking, because you are putting the incomplete portion of a current task on hold momentarily, then picking up where you left off. This involves the executive function of *working memory*, which helps you manage interruptions by keeping the current task in mind so you can return to it. Working memory works in conjunction with short-term memory, acting as the buffer that allows for the organization and manipulation of information that is being stored for short-term.

Although people with autism tend to remember a great deal of information, many of them have poor working memory. An employee on the spectrum may find it difficult to continue a task that was temporarily put on hold, because he does not have a "pause" button and may lose the thread of what he was doing when interrupted, and he may need to start the task from the beginning (see Figure 9.3).

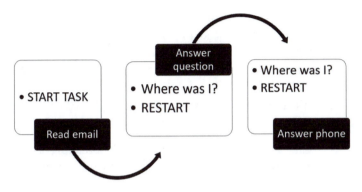

Figure 9.3: Effect of interruptions on individuals with autism

Business research suggests that it takes a person anywhere from 2 to 15 minutes to reorient himself to what he was working on before the interruption,[48] so even periodically checking email can take its toll on neuro-typicals as well as individuals on the spectrum. According to Gloria Mark, an "interruption scientist" at the University of California, there is a "cognitive cost" to an interruption, because it can change the physical layout of your environment.[49] For example, when someone asks you for information, you may need to open new windows on your computer or place papers you have been handed on your desk. For individuals on the spectrum, the change in their physical environment may make it more difficult for them to reconstruct what they were doing before the interruption, so they need to go back and redo work already completed.

How do you deal with an employee who can't multitask?

Today's workplace depends on juggling many tasks at once. Although multitasking is not as productive as one might believe, many employees rely on rapidly shifting between activities to get through their workload. Individuals on the autism spectrum tend to concentrate deeply or *hyperfocus* when working on a task, often to the exclusion of everything else. Pulling their focus away from one thing and putting it on another takes a great deal of energy, so minimize the amount of transitioning they need to do. Whenever possible, allow the employee to complete a task before moving to another one by scheduling enough time for the task, as well as time to transition.

Organization and planning will make it easier for an employee to deal with multiple tasks:

- Make a large task more manageable by breaking it down into a sequence of smaller steps that can be completed individually.

- Use a wall calendar to divide each task into color-coded time slots.

- Use inbox-style trays to hold notes and paperwork for each task.

- Jot down notes needed for continuing the work before switching to a different task.

To minimize interruptions, allow the employee to let phone calls go to voicemail, and then designate a block of time exclusively for handling emails and returning phone calls. If you need to interrupt an employee, give him time to break away from what he was doing.

Related material

- Section 9.1

- Chapter 8: Organization

Time management:
Accommodations summary

Time management is an *executive function* issue, because it involves how you *organize* your time and understand the *passage* of time. Some people on the autism spectrum are very organized and have no trouble meeting deadlines, while others have difficulties with scheduling. One's ability to manage time is determined by the ability to estimate the amount of time needed to complete a project (*planning*, discussed in Chapter 8); to shift gears and *transition* to another task; to begin a task (*initiating*, discussed in Chapter 8); to know when to stop (*hyperfocus*); to monitor and evaluate one's own performance; as well as processing speed.

Processing speed is not an executive function, or related to intelligence, but it is an important factor in effective time management. Regulating your processing speed allows you to control how slowly or quickly you perform a task, based upon its relative importance and time frame. Employees on the spectrum who appear to have slow processing speed may:

- be overwhelmed by too much information at once

- need more time to make decisions or give answers

- have trouble executing instructions when multiple requests are made at the same time.

Individuals with autism tend to become absorbed in tasks that they find stimulating and rewarding. This style of thinking, called *hyperfocus*, involves very deep, concentrated thought, and is pleasurable for the person doing it. Hyperfocus may cause an employee to become so immersed in a task that he becomes oblivious to everything else going on around him, resulting in time management issues and problems shifting to and completing other assigned tasks. It can be especially difficult for someone on the spectrum when employees are expected to *multitask*.

Lastly, employees on the spectrum may need to repeat work if interrupted, due to challenges with working memory. Although they remember large amounts of information, they may struggle organizing that information and remembering where they were in an assignment if faced with constant interruptions.

Your effective use of time at work is influenced by many things, including your organizational abilities, your processing speed, your working memory, and your work environment. Employees on the autism spectrum may need help managing their time due to challenges with:

- transitioning

- being intensely focused (*hyperfocus*)

- managing multiple tasks.

Strategies for addressing time management are not limited to individuals on the autism spectrum; the field of *coaching* was initially developed in the corporate setting to help people work more effectively by addressing some of the executive function issues discussed in this section.

Effective time management involves accurately estimating how much time a task will take, deciding how to divide your time throughout the day, moving from one task to another, and planning how to meet deadlines. Give employees on the spectrum clear guidelines about assignments:

- Be specific about deadlines and time frames, including To Do lists.

- Provide the *context of time* to help the employee know how much time the task requires and how the work will fit into the time that he has available.

- Give an indication of the scope and depth expected within the allotted time and the level of priority.

- Schedule regular meetings to review progress on long-term projects and practice adjusting deadlines based on progress.

- Use technology, smartphones, and electronic calendars to schedule appointments with reminders and set alarms.

Transitioning:

- Give an employee on the spectrum a break between tasks so he can fully extract himself from one task before starting on another.

- Suggest physical movement, such as a quick walk down the hall, to help the employee make a mental break from a completed task, so he can start on the next one.

- Ask specific questions, such as "Once you completed this task, how long did it take you to get started on the next one?" or "Are there specific times of day or types of tasks when shifting gears is the most challenging for you?" to identify problem areas of transitioning for an employee.

- Review the schedule in advance, so the employee will be mentally prepared for transitions that need to occur.

Some individuals on the spectrum become so absorbed in their work that they lose track of time. Additionally, individuals on the spectrum do not have a "pause button," and if they are interrupted may need to go back to the beginning of a task. Structure and advance notice are very helpful for employees with autism in dealing with constantly changing demands of their job.

- Set a timer so the employee knows when to complete one task and move on to another.

- Minimize the amount of transitioning they need to do in their job.

- Schedule sufficient time for the employee to complete the task assigned before needing to move on to another assignment.

Managing multiple tasks:

- Break larger tasks down into smaller segments that can be completed individually.

- Use inbox-style trays to hold notes and paperwork for each task.

- Use a wall calendar to divide each task into color-coded time slots.

Interruptions:

- Allow the employee to complete a task before asking him to move on to another, if at all possible.

- Jot down notes needed for continuing assignments that have to be stopped and picked up at a later time before switching to a new task.

- Minimize interruptions by scheduling time during the day for emails and phone calls.

- Provide a short notice that you will need to interrupt the employee from what they are doing, if possible.

Chapter 10

WORK QUALITY

Part Two discusses the *social challenges* in the workplace that employees on the autism spectrum face, while the first two chapters of Part Three focus on the *work performance* issues that present difficulties for these individuals. *Both* of these areas combine when evaluating the work quality of employees on the spectrum in areas such as understanding the goals of the task, anticipating the needs of a manager, interpreting instructions, evaluating different approaches, changing strategy, and accepting advice and feedback. We all ask ourselves questions when beginning a new assignment. For individuals on the spectrum, the ability to answer those questions and effectively complete the assignment is significantly influenced by the concepts discussed in this book and listed in Figure 10.1

What do I need to do?	**Theory of mind**
How should I do it?	**Literal thinking**
Who do I work with?	**Seeing the "big picture"**
What should it look like?	**Office politics**
Am I doing it correctly?	**Working memory**
Should I do it differently?	**Planning**
Do I need help?	**Prioritization**
Have I done this before?	**Time management**
	Generalization
	Initiation
	Flexibility
	Transitioning
	Self-monitoring

Figure 10.1: The influence of cognitive factors on work quality

For most employees, work-quality issues are mainly concentrated in the area of executive functioning (i.e. *organizational skills*), and not viewed as related to social interaction. However, for an employee on the autism spectrum, the ability to do his job effectively may have as much to do with communication and theory of mind as it does with the ability to plan and prioritize. More importantly, the perception of how well an employee with autism does his job is not only based on his *aptitude* (i.e. his ability to deliver the work), it also involves the *attitude* he has about the work as well as working with others.

In this chapter, we will cover the most commonly perceived work-quality challenges for individuals on the spectrum, including interpreting work requests, learning from prior assignments, flexibility, and dealing with feedback and criticism. Although we the use term "manager" throughout this discussion, it can to refer to anyone in a supervisory or mentoring position.

On a positive note:

- While inflexibility in some areas may be an issue for employees on the spectrum, their adherence to policies and procedures and ability to notice non-compliance and such can be a valuable risk-management tool for organizations.

- Many individuals with autism have come up with new and creative ways of solving problems because they do not adhere to the conventional ways of doing things.

As you read this chapter, please remember that not all individuals with autism will display all the behaviors discussed. Each individual on the spectrum is different, and their challenges related to autism will be unique to them.

Section 10.1: How many times do I have to tell him?

Topics covered

- Does not anticipate your needs

- Does not deliver what you have asked for

- Interprets instructions too literally

- Forgets what he's told to do

- Does not learn from prior assignments

- Needs constant feedback

Are you seeing these behaviors?

- An employee is responsible for the same task every month, and every month it needs to be re-explained. *And you think to yourself, "How many times do I need to tell him?"*

- You go over a list of things to do for the day with an employee, only to find that he has forgotten half of them.

What are the underlying issues?
Work performance and theory of mind

Successfully completing tasks involves understanding the goals of the person assigning the work, as well as what he expects the outcome to look like; however, employees are not always mind readers. A busy manager may delegate what she considers a straightforward assignment to an employee without much explanation. However, when the work is returned, it bears little resemblance to what she expected.

Because of problems with *theory of mind* (discussed in Part Two) people on the spectrum have difficulty viewing a situation from another person's perspective, so they may struggle with anticipating what a manager or colleague might want or need. They may be oblivious to the shorthand of facial expressions, tone of voice, or body language that signals important information about the context or extenuating circumstances of the assignment.

For example, a manager under pressure might tell an employee responsible for a marketing report, "My boss is fuming because he needed the report yesterday!" The manager assumes that her tone of voice signals that the employee should go to his cubicle, stop any other task, and immediately begin work on the report. However, an individual on the spectrum is likely to interpret the manager's statement separate from its emotional context. He mistakenly concludes that since yesterday has passed, there is no need to do the report, and continues with other assignments. The manager would have been more successful giving a direct, specific request, such as, "Stop your other work and bring me the marketing report by 3 P.M."

An employee with autism may interpret instructions literally because he lacks the cognitive flexibility to consider the request in *context*. For example, when a manager says to an employee, "Do the sales report the same way you did it last month," she expects the employee to take aspects of the task that are the same (e.g. the format and the source of the data) and fill it in with the information that is *not* the same (e.g. the sales figures for the current month). Because his mind tends toward the perception of details and differences rather than similarities, an employee on the spectrum may not know how to proceed when something changes, such as an additional set of sales figures from new markets.

Keep in mind that an employee with autism may not volunteer important information unless you directly request it, because he may assume you know what he is thinking!

"If you want something, say it. Don't beat around the bush."

Clear communication about projects and tasks will benefit every employee, and it is essential for those on the spectrum. There are three components to any request; vagueness or false assumptions in any of these areas can affect the successful completion of a task or project, especially for a person with autism. To ensure a successful outcome, the employee needs to know the specific details and parameters of the work assigned (*What do I need to do?*); how to process and interpret the request (*How am I going to do it?*); and the expected work product (*What do I need to deliver?*), as represented in Figure 10.2.

Figure 10.2: Components of a work request

Individuals on the spectrum are most comfortable and productive when they have rules and a structure to follow, so any work assignment should include specifics about what outcome you expect, and why it is important, as well as any samples of work that are similar in format and structure. Specifically list important details such as, "It needs to include X and Y," explain what priorities the project has relative to other work, and the time frame in which it should be delivered. Allow an individual with autism extra time to process what you say to him, and check that he has understood your needs by asking him to repeat the instructions back to you. Plan dates to review interim pieces of work, or assign a colleague to check in with the employee regularly.

"If I'm doing something wrong, tell me, and I won't be offended."

Working memory

Employees on the spectrum take pride in their work, so if you assigned a task verbally and it has not been completed (or it is not what you expect), it is important to find out the cause: Were the instructions not clear? Does he have difficulty planning how to proceed (see Chapter 8)? Or did he forget what you said? *Working memory* is an executive function that refers to the ability to hold information in memory over a short period of time, such as remembering all the things someone tells you to do. Individuals on the autism spectrum have an excellent memory for detail, but some may have problems with working memory (i.e. keeping ideas in mind while using them to complete tasks and solve problems).

A person with poor working memory may become overwhelmed if he is given too much information at once, and may not be able to follow multi-step verbal instructions. For example, if you tell an employee five things he needs to do on a project, the less recent ones may not be retained, and he may just remember the last thing he heard. If an employee asks obvious questions after receiving instructions, it may be due to poor working memory, rather than not paying attention.

Learning from prior assignments

Working memory also incorporates drawing on past learning or experience and applying that to a current situation. A manager generally assumes that if an employee has worked on a prior assignment, he will know how to approach an assignment that is similar. Transfer of learning, or *generalization*, happens when you focus on the features that are *similar* in two situations, rather than what is unique to each one. Without generalization, you would need to start at "square one" for every task, because even minor differences would make every task different. Finding past solutions based on experience and using them as a template when working on something new for the first time saves a great deal of time and energy in the workplace.

Individuals on the spectrum may not intuitively learn from prior assignments, because they are more likely to focus on what is *different* than on what is the same. They do not think of tasks or assignments as template-based, where there is a similarity between something they have done before and what they need to do now. However, an employee with autism *can* learn to generalize if he is given a framework or examples of what the work product should look like, so that he has a means for comparison. Give guidance, stressing the similarities and suggesting how to deal with any differences, so he can incorporate that as a rule for future tasks of the same type.

It is always important to make sure that any employee is in the appropriate job, and a person on the spectrum may not be the right candidate for a job that requires constant decision-making or where every assignment is completely different with little guidance. However, he may be able to handle these demands in areas that are inherently more structured, such as engineering, programming, finance, and technology, or one where he has in-depth expertise, such as medicine, research, law, and filmmaking to name a few.

Self-monitoring

Day to day we all make small adjustments in working toward the goals that we have. *Self-monitoring* is the executive function the allows you to keep track of and monitor your performance on a task and give yourself feedback, by stepping back and assessing how you are meeting your goals. We adjust our strategies, spot errors, and change the speed at which we work in response to this self-feedback.

A person with strong self-monitoring will build confidence and need less direct supervision, as his perception of how he is doing matches the quality of his work. Because people on the spectrum struggle with monitoring and assessing their progress in *context*, an employee may not know if an assignment is on track, and he may not feel confident in his work. On the other hand, he may be surprised by a poor evaluation or negative feedback, if he assumed that his work was meeting expectations. People who struggle with self-monitoring may also find it hard to do routine tasks well when stressed or under pressure, to detect mistakes in their work, to learn new tasks quickly, or to do a familiar task well in an unfamiliar environment.

An important component of self-monitoring is paying attention to one's own "self-talk" or inner voice; that is, what we think or say to ourselves while solving problems, working on tasks, or going through a mental check list. Research has shown that self-talk helps us work more productively, accurately, and confidently, and can even help regulate emotions.[50] In the workplace, *instructional self-talk* in particular can be very effective, such as guiding oneself through the steps of a task or weighing out the pros and cons of a decision.

For employees on the spectrum, self-talk may strengthen their ability to self-monitor by helping them internalize the guidance they receive from managers and colleagues. It can serve many functions when working through an assignment, such as defining the nature and demands of a task, maintaining focus and generating a game plan, using a strategy, detecting and correcting errors, and dealing with any problems that arise.[51]

Helping an employee engage in self-talk as a means of monitoring his work can be as simple as suggesting he *silently* talk himself through a task by using step-by-step reminders at each phase. Self-talk should be direct, specific, and positive. For example, when writing a memo, an employee might give himself silent reminders, such as "First I need to pick out the most important point and put that at the top." It is interesting to note that, although one can use either "I" or "you" when self-talking, current research suggests that using "you" tends to be more objective and effective, similar to giving someone else helpful feedback or advice.[52, 53]

Feedback

Most people know if they are on the right track by paying attention to internal checkpoints, but an employee on the spectrum may need external feedback from a manager or colleague to be assured they are doing something correctly, or because they are not fully confident in the final output required. The employee's anxiety about not wanting to be wrong may also play a part, which can intensify if he asks for feedback and is not sure when he will receive it.

If a manager sees that an employee's work product is in the right direction, then a constant request for feedback may be related to anxiety or confidence, and it is appropriate to set a time to meet that is not immediate. Questions that indicate a lack of clarity, however, need to be addressed as soon as possible, because an individual with autism may not be able to continue *any* part of the project if a smaller part of it is not clear. Keep in mind that an individual with poor self-monitoring might think his work is on target when it is not and may resist advice or overreact to criticism (discussed in Chapter 6 and Section 10.2). However, if a request for feedback is initiated by the employee himself, it generally indicates that he is seeking help, advice, or reassurance.

> *"I think the most important thing you can do for a person with Asperger's is to give feedback. Be straight and tell it like it really is. You may feel uncomfortable giving that information, but without the true knowledge of what they need to do, they're not going to be able to do it."*

For some people, the constant requirement for feedback can be addressed by putting together a structured schedule for feedback sessions, which eliminates the uncertainty of when feedback will be coming.

How do you deal with an employee who repeatedly needs to be told what to do?

It is only natural to get impatient when you need to explain something repeatedly to an employee because he has forgotten what you told him or does not complete a task to your specifications. Whenever an employee on the autism spectrum seems to miss what is clearly obvious, remember: It is obvious to *you*.

Individuals with autism have a strong work ethic and the desire to do the best job possible, but they may have difficulty "reading your mind" (i.e. anticipating your goals and needs). As discussed previously, uncertainty can arise from vague requests or difficulties in processing instructions. Feeling unsure about a task may be anxiety-provoking, so they may constantly ask questions and request feedback.

When you assign a task to an employee on the spectrum that is similar to one he has completed in the past, supply a template or a copy of the completed work product whenever possible, so he can refer to it. If he is not sure how to proceed, ask him to identify what is the *same* about the two tasks, so he can view the new task as a version of the prior one, then work with him to make adjustments based on the *differences*. Keep in mind that an individual with autism may see contingencies that other people may miss or not deem relevant. Acknowledging his concern will help alleviate any anxiety he may feel when a template or prior work does not apply exactly to a current task.

When an employee does not deliver what you have asked for, it may seem that he was not paying attention; however, he may have difficulties with working memory and processing speed. When assigning tasks to an employee with autism, be specific and allow him to takes notes so he will have a written record of your request. If it is difficult for him to listen while taking notes, allow him to record the conversation—there are apps for tablets and electronic pens that will sync the recording with what he writes, for easy playback and review. If bad penmanship is an issue, he may be more efficient taking notes with an iPad or keyboard.

As discussed above, it is important that you be as specific as possible when you delegate work to employees on the spectrum. Assume that any request you make may be taken literally, so do not rely on facial expressions or figurative and inexact language. Below are some guidelines for delegating work:

- Explain what *outcome* you need and why.

- List the *details* that you care about. An individual on the spectrum may not be able to anticipate what *parameters* he should keep in mind, so address those with him before he begins the assignment.

- Provide *samples* of what you expect, if possible.

- Give a specific *deadline* or *time frame* and explain the *level of priority* relative to the employee's schedule.

- Give the employee enough *time to process* what you say to him, and then ask him to repeat back to you his understanding of the details, and clarify if necessary. Encourage him to create a checklist for reference as he works on the task.

Suggestions and offers to help the individual should be specific as well, such as "When I give you these assignments, what would make it easier for you to remember everything?" or "I want to go over the details of the project with you, so you may want to record our conversation on your phone."

An individual with autism may ask a great deal of questions about the details of assignments because he wants to know what is expected of him. Structure will help keep the amount and frequency of questions in check. A manager can set up specific times to meet and ask the individual to hold on to certain questions until that time. When an employee needs immediate feedback because he is stuck, suggest that he ask a question via email or see a specific colleague for clarification. If the employee is working on a large report, ask to see a draft or interim data, or assign a colleague to check in with him as the work unfolds.

Although an individual on the spectrum may have difficulties observing his own progress as he works on a task, you can encourage self-monitoring by having him refer to checklists and milestones. "Self-talking" silently is helpful for problem-solving or following procedures as an employee works through a project.

Related material

- Section 10.2

- Chapter 6: Social Interaction

Section 10.2: What an attitude!

Topics covered

- Does only what is asked of him, nothing more

- Does what he wants, rather than what is asked

- Questions the value of assigned tasks

- Does not ask for clarification

- Resists advice or overreacts to criticism

- Walks around the office for no apparent reason

Are you seeing these behaviors?

- Every time you ask an employee to do something differently, he argues with you. *And you think to yourself, "What an attitude!"*

- An employee's work demonstrates that he needs assistance, yet he never asks for help.

- You are sitting in a meeting and notice an employee walking past the conference room every 15 minutes, and you wonder, "Where is he going all the time?"

What's the underlying issue?
Attitude vs. aptitude

Our impression of an employee's attitude toward his work often influences how well we think he is doing his job. It's a natural assumption, when an employee does only what he has been asked to do or insists on doing things "his way," that he does not care about the job or has a "bad attitude." However, when dealing with an individual on the spectrum, these assumptions may not be warranted, because his attitude and behavior might be due to some of the challenges of being on the spectrum.

Employees who are *proactive* are highly valued in the workplace, because they go beyond the requirements of their job, while those who do only what they have been assigned and nothing more, are generally characterized as "unmotivated." Individuals on the autism spectrum may have difficulty understanding the politics of the workplace regarding advancing one's career and being proactive: that the workplace is an environment where, if you have finished an assignment, you are expected to ask for more work. Because of their tendency toward literal thinking and missing the "big picture," they may not anticipate what other work needs to be done. Consequently, they might appear to lack initiative, which can affect their chances for advancement. Conversely, they may believe certain work should be done and go ahead and do it without asking, not realizing that management is holding off on certain projects for reasons not apparent to them. Although professionals on the spectrum may not seem to be motivated by promotions or a bigger paycheck, they do care very much about their jobs, and want to perform well and be recognized for their contributions.

What we think of as *proactive* behavior involves executive functions such as *self-monitoring*, *planning*, and *initiation*, as well as *theory of mind* and the ability to see one's work as *part of a larger whole*. It is actually a complex set of actions that may prove difficult for an employee on the spectrum. He needs to:

- know that he has finished his assignment
- anticipate what work his manager might want him to do next (or refer to a list)
- start to do the next task, or
- report to his manager and ask for the next assignment.

A person on the spectrum, however, who thinks literally, may simply conclude that once he completes the task he was asked to do, he should just wait for his next assignment. Similarly, an employee with time management issues may think he is being productive when he rushes to do a week's worth of work in two days, then sits with nothing to do for the rest of the week. A supervisor, seeing an employee sit idly, is likely to think, "Why is he doing nothing?" and might conclude that the individual is wasting time or not doing his job.

A team member on the spectrum who has been assigned a task that depends on work from another team member may sit and wait for that work to be completed, because he does not understand the bigger picture (i.e. the *context*) that other team tasks may be dependent on the completion of *his* work. He may not be aware that it is appropriate politely to ask when he can expect the work, offer assistance, or explain the situation to the team leader.

Inflexibility

> *"People on the spectrum, we like our routines. We like to continue doing things the same way."*

Inflexibility is part of being on the spectrum; an employee with autism may appear to do what he wants, rather than what he has been asked to do. *Cognitive flexibility* is the executive function that allows us to shift thinking or attention in response to context, and adapt to changing conditions. An employee who struggles with flexibility may have difficulties with:

- interpreting information in multiple ways and understanding that there is more than one way to accomplish a task

- using new strategies to solve problems

- changing routines

- stopping one activity to begin another

- accepting help from others.

Black-and-white thinking is associated with lack of flexibility, as is the rigid adherence to rules and routines. Flexible thinking requires the ability to "unlearn" old ways of doing things, but many individuals on the spectrum resist change in general (discussed in Chapter 11). For example, an employee may appear to be stubborn because he gets stuck on a small detail or part of a routine and resists advice, or refuses to use a workaround solution; so what appears as inflexibility is really his difficulty transitioning to a new way of thinking or different expectation.

As discussed in Chapter 9, individuals on the spectrum tend to focus intensely, or *hyperfocus*, especially with something they are interested in. Because of this singular focus, an employee may get caught up in a detail that is not relevant or go off on a tangent and not realize that he is no longer on task.

The two sides of context

As mentioned previously, people with autism find it difficult to shift their attention and change their reactions in response to circumstances, so an individual may not consider how *his* work fits within the *context* of what needs to be done to achieve the goals of his workplace. Because of challenges with flexibility, an employee may become locked into black-and-white thinking, where there is a *right* way to do something (his way) or a *wrong* way (what he has been asked to do). An individual with autism who feels he is always right may prefer to work alone, rather than deal with input from others or justify his thinking.

For example, an employee on the spectrum may push back if he feels that the way he has been asked to perform an assignment will lead to errors or is inefficient. He may insist on changing the process or a formula, without considering the broader consequences for the people and departments who depend on the results of his work. As you will recall from previous chapters, many people with autism struggle seeing the "big picture," so it is important to explain the broader context of *why* something cannot be changed, and give the employee a rule that he should not change anything without approval from his supervisor or manager.

Likewise, an employee might question the value of an assigned task or complain about working on it, because he may not grasp the task's relevance or perceive how it fits into the greater scheme of things. Respond to such push-back by providing the bigger picture (the *context*) of why he's doing the task, or explaining that requests by someone further up the chain are not subject to debate.

Keep in mind that sometimes *not* relying on context can be a benefit. An employee on the spectrum may have a fresh perspective on solving a problem or doing an analysis, because he will not be influenced by convention, office politics, or the status quo. Individuals with autism at times might produce unexpected results or proceed in an unorthodox manner, which can lead to unique and creative solutions.

For example, researchers studying the relationship of autism to divergent ("out-of-the-box") thinking found that people with autistic traits may approach creativity problems in a different way by going directly to less common ideas. They asked participants to come up with as many alternative uses as they could for a paper clip. People with higher levels of autistic traits provided more unusual and creative responses, such as a weight on a paper airplane; a wire to support cut flowers; a counter/token for game/gambling; and a light duty spring. More common responses included a hook or pin; a tool for cleaning small grooves and for making jewelry.[54]

Highly creative and unconventional individuals on the spectrum include TV garden designer Alan Gardner (*The*

Autistic Gardener), British architectural artist Stephen Wiltshire, and American author and professor of animal science, Temple Grandin.

Asking for help

As discussed in Section 10.1, some employees with autism may constantly ask for feedback due to anxiety or lack of confidence, or because they did not understand an assignment. On the other hand, an employee with autism may be reluctant to ask for help or clarification because he does not want to be perceived as being incapable, or has been chided for asking "obvious questions" in the past. People on the spectrum who have struggled to find and retain jobs may be fearful of revealing that they need help, and therefore may not come forward with questions, despite wanting to do their best. This may especially be an issue for entry-level or new employees, who may not understand that an initial learning period is expected, and that there is nothing wrong with asking questions that one cannot answer oneself.

Distractions

Once someone is assigned a task, the expectation is that he will go back to his desk and work on it. Although it is appropriate to take short breaks during the workday, when an individual constantly walks around the office, we assume that he is not doing his job or is easily distracted.

There are several reasons why an individual on the spectrum may take frequent breaks, such as the need to physically move about to aid in transitioning (discussed in Chapter 9). An employee may also not know how to fill unstructured time, and walk around because he has nothing else to do, or take breaks too frequently because he is not aware of the passage of time. Also, an employee struggling to begin or initiate a task (discussed in Chapter 8), but afraid to ask directly for help, may be looking for a way to get attention from a manager or colleague to engage their help in getting started.

Sensitivity to the noises of the workplace can be a major distraction to an employee on the spectrum. For example, the whirring of the copy machine might cause him to totally lose his focus, so he may frequently leave his desk to escape the noise. The sensory aspects of the workplace will be discussed in Part Four: Sensory Challenges.

How do you deal with an employee who has a bad attitude?

Generally, when addressing issues of an employee's work performance, providing feedback and expectations of responsibilities and the consequences of not meeting performance standards is sufficient. However, for an employee on the autism spectrum, this type of intervention alone may not be suitable, because of the combined effect of challenges with social interactions and difficulties in executive functioning.

Issues related to the hidden curriculum, theory of mind, and seeing the "big picture" are all related to the work quality of an individual with autism, because they affect how he interprets work assignments and carries them out. If an employee on the spectrum seems to be "doing nothing," do not assume that he is not motivated to do a good job, as it may be due to his not knowing what to do after he has finished a task. Being proactive requires anticipating a manager's goals and needs, which may be difficult for an individual with autism. To help him fill up free time, maintain a list of projects in order of priority, with an estimate of how much time is needed. Create a rule that when he is finished with a task, he should evaluate how much free time he has, then move down the list of additional things that need to be done until he finds one that fits the time available. If necessary, he can ask his manager for another assignment. If poor time management results in rushing through his work, have him break the assignment into slots of time that are spread out over the week.

An employee may sit idly if he is waiting for work to be completed from a team member, because he may not realize that it is appropriate to do other work in the interim, or speak to the team member. Prompt him to go to his supervisor and explain that he cannot proceed without the work and ask if there is anything else he should do. He can also go to his teammate and say, "I need this before I can finish my work, is there something I can do to help you get it done?"

If inflexibility is an issue with an individual with autism, stress the *context* of the situation, so he can see how his actions fit into a broader scheme. For example, an employee might detect what he perceives to be an error in a process, procedure, or formula that he has been asked to follow, and may be compelled to change it without regard for how that change may affect work by other colleagues. First, acknowledge his concerns (after all, he may be correct!), then explain *why* the change is not appropriate: if a process that is used broadly throughout the organization changes, the work may not consolidate properly at the end. Set a rule that he should not make any changes to procedures on his own, and that he should consult a supervisor before making changes of any kind. An employee might also resist doing a task that he feels is not relevant. If he asks why he has been asked to do something; again, provide the context (i.e. the bigger picture of how his work will be used).

Many individuals on the spectrum regard asking for help or clarification as a sign of weakness or being too dependent; others may fear that they will be seen as not knowing how to do their job. However, asking for guidance may help the individual realize that he was doing things that were unnecessary, or that he was spending time on an activity that was not relevant to the project. If you suspect that an employee needs help but is reluctant to ask for it, you can ask him to explain the process in question, and then offer suggestions.

The black-and-white, all-or-none thinking of an individual with autism may make accepting criticism difficult, as he may feel that the entire project is faulty and should be scrapped. When delivering constructive criticism, stress what has been done correctly first, then ease into the rest. If he is hard on himself, explain that even a genius can make a mistake, and then help him develop a rule to follow to guard against the mistake happening again.

When you see an employee wandering about the office, it may be that he needs a physical break in order to transition, or it may be due to sensory issues, such as a noisy environment (covered in Chapter 11). Time management may also be a problem, and an employee on the spectrum may not know how to fill unstructured time or how frequently to take a break. For example, an employee who is not fully aware of the passage of time may leave his office to take a break every 15 minutes. However, if a manager schedules a ten-minute break every hour, the employee will be able to stay at his desk, because he knows that the break is coming. Lastly, the employee may be having trouble starting his assignment, but be afraid to ask for help. Ask the employee if he is having difficulty with any aspect of his current assignment and needs some immediate assistance.

Related material

- Section 10.1

- Chapter 5: Talking

- Chapter 8: Organization

- Chapter 9: Time Management

- Chapter 11: Emotional Regulation

Work quality: Accommodations summary

An individual's *aptitude* and *attitude* are important factors in how an employer evaluates an employee's work quality. How many times have you worked with someone where you have thought "I wish you could read my mind" or "How many times do I have to tell you" or "Boy, what an attitude"? The aptitude and attitude of people with autism can be impacted by challenges related to the hidden curriculum and theory of mind (discussed in Chapter 5) and executive functioning (discussed in Chapter 8). Understanding how these challenges may affect work performance and attitude is key to giving employees on the spectrum the tools to perform to the best of their ability.

Employees with autism take pride in their jobs and want to deliver high-quality work consistently. However, their neurological makeup and cognitive style may cause them to miss the "big picture" because they tend to focus on the details and differences, making it difficult for them to anticipate your expectations or intuitively learn from prior assignments. As a result, they may be anxious or lack confidence about meeting expectations, and seek frequent feedback.

Employers look for employees to be proactive in the workplace and flexible in taking on new assignments that may change with the organization's broader goals. People with autism tend to thrive on structure and are most comfortable with explicit expectations. When faced with uncertainty or significant change, they may cling to rules and routines or their point of view. If they become anxious, they may reject feedback or not ask for help, for fear of being perceived as unable to do their job.

Employers can benefit from the high-quality work that employees on the spectrum are able to deliver, as long as they understand that individuals with autism are not displaying a disregard for their job or colleagues if they struggle with:

- generalizing information
- self-monitoring
- being flexible
- asking for help
- accepting feedback.

Keep in mind that many people on the spectrum have struggled to obtain and maintain employment, and can become exceptionally anxious when they believe their work quality does not meet expectations. By working with them to alleviate this anxiety, you can have a major impact on their ability to perform to their greatest capability.

An employee may have trouble starting or completing a task that is *similar* to a previous one, because details such as information and procedures have been changed, added, or eliminated. With prompting, however, the employee can eventually learn to handle these minor differences.

- Include specifics about what outcome you expect, and why it is important, as well as any samples of work that are in a similar format and structure for assignments.

- When assigning tasks that are similar, ask the employee to identify what is the *same* about the two tasks, so he can view the new task as a version of the prior one, then work with him to make adjustments based on the *differences*.

- Allow him to takes notes so he will have a written record of your request. If it is difficult for him to listen while taking notes, allow him to record the conversation.

Self-monitoring:

- Address questions related to lack of clarity as soon as possible.

- Suggest an employee ask questions via email or see a specific colleague for clarification.

- Put together a schedule for regular feedback sessions, eliminating the uncertainty around when the employee can expect feedback.

- Encourage the employee to refer to checklists and preset milestones to self-monitor his progress.

The perception of how well an employee does his job is based on his *attitude* toward the work and his colleagues as much as it is on his *aptitude* for that work. Employees with autism may need structure and coaching to ensure they don't project the wrong attitude at work.

- Acknowledge the employee's concerns, and then explain the broader context of *why* something cannot be changed, or should be changed, or needs to be done, if an employee on the spectrum is resistant.

- Provide rules about what decisions/changes the employee can make alone versus needing to check with a supervisor.

Asking for help:

- Ask the employee to explain their work and then offer suggestions if they tend not to ask questions.

- Let the employee know that it is natural to have questions, and set aside structured times specifically for the employee to ask those questions.

- Practice brainstorming with the employee, focusing on asking questions and entertaining ideas of others.

Accepting feedback:

- Stress what has been done correctly first, when delivering constructive criticism.

- Explain that everyone makes mistakes and it is an expected part of learning on the job.

- Help the employee develop rules to follow in the future to prevent similar mistakes from occurring.

- Provide feedback in real time and at regularly scheduled times. Do not skip feedback meetings, even when the feedback is only positive.

Chapter 11

EMOTIONAL REGULATION

An important executive function skill is *emotional regulation*—the ability to control how we express our emotions. Everyone has problems with regulating emotions from time to time, but individuals on the spectrum have additional challenges because of their social, sensory, and cognitive issues, as well as difficulties recognizing their own emotional state.

According to psychologist Lynda Geller, an expert in workplace and social issues for people on the autism spectrum, emotional regulation affects more than just how we feel:

> Emotions are often thought to be only feeling states, but they are much more than that… They play a critical role in regulating important processes including memory, perception, attention, and physical response. Emotional regulation includes the processes whereby we influence which emotions we have, when we have them, and how we experience and express them.[55]

Emotional regulation allows us to control how much emotion we let out, similar to a pressure valve. By contrast, individuals with autism tend to have only an on/off switch, which may result in an emotional reaction that is out of proportion to the situation that triggered it. Most people can regulate their emotions by thinking about a situation from another perspective or doing something else as a distraction, but these strategies may be difficult for an employee on the spectrum.

Additionally, difficulties with emotional regulation can affect how well an employee on the spectrum manages anxiety, deals with change, and keeps from "losing it" when frustrations build.

In this chapter, we will cover the most common issues related to emotional regulation for employees on the autism spectrum, including dealing with anxiety, change, emotional control, and emotional exhaustion.

On a positive note:

- Learning to reduce anxiety in your workplace in general benefits *all* employees.

- While individuals with autism may have difficulty dealing with a lot of change, they have a high tolerance for jobs that others may find repetitive.

As you read this chapter, please remember that not all individuals with autism will display all the behaviors discussed. Each individual on the spectrum is different, and their challenges related to autism will be unique to them.

Section 11.1: Everything seems to bother him!

Topics covered

- Appears overly anxious
- Gets upset over changes in schedule and staff
- Easily frustrated by interruptions and minor changes in daily routine
- Overreacts to others' emotions
- Distorts the magnitude of a situation

Are you seeing these behaviors?

- You hand an employee a small task to do, and he goes into a 20-minute monologue about how you do not respect his time... *And you think to yourself, "Everything seems to bother him!"*
- A team member is upset that a meeting has been pushed back 15 minutes.

What are the underlying issues?

While an individual with autism may appear to get upset over seemingly minor things, there are real reasons behind it. Many things can cause an employee on the spectrum to overreact emotionally or become anxious, frustrated, or irritated; often there is no apparent "trigger," rather it is the cumulative effect of small situations. Even the physical environment can take its toll on the individual, as we will discuss in Part Four: Sensory Challenges. Whatever the source, keep in mind that many of these issues are not within the employee's control, and he is not deliberately trying to be stubborn or contrary.

Anxiety

Anxiety creates one of the biggest challenges for individuals on the autism spectrum. We all need a certain amount of anxiety to keep ourselves focused, but as anxiety builds, we can no longer concentrate on the task at hand and become distracted by the emotions resulting from our anxiety.

Many of the workplace situations that create anxiety for an employee with autism have been discussed in the previous chapters, such as:

- not understanding what is expected of him

- not operating as quickly or as efficiently as expected

- receiving demands from multiple people at the same time

- receiving criticism.

An employee may also worry about not doing a good job or being terminated, especially if he is new to the workforce or has been terminated in the past. In addition, an individual on the spectrum may feel anxious when someone exhibits strong emotions or when he anticipates his own loss of emotional control, discussed later in this section. Sensory challenges, such as being exposed to excessive noise, harsh office lighting, and other sensory inputs (covered in Part Four), can also raise anxiety levels.

An employee with autism may have difficulty interpreting his own emotions and might not recognize that he is becoming overwhelmed during the early stages, so it is important to intervene if you notice that the person is becoming anxious or agitated. Additionally, when an individual with autism worries over something work-related, he may not have the same ability as his colleagues to de-stress.

Social gatherings often are the source of anxiety for many people on the spectrum; they may want to avoid unintentionally breaking hidden curriculum rules, but may have trouble determining which rules apply.

Dealing with change

Dealing with changes in routines or schedules can also make individuals on the spectrum anxious. Change can be challenging for anyone, and it is easy to become out of sorts because of an interruption in routine. Many of us develop coping skills to help deal with change, but sudden change can still take us off guard. For many businesses, change is one of the few things that can be counted on, and employees learn to cope with shifting schedules, priorities, and procedures. However, for people on the spectrum, change can be challenging to deal with and deeply unsettling, as it is harder for them to understand that, in the workplace, things do not flow in a natural order or as expected.

The world can seem a very unpredictable and confusing place to people with autism, so the consistency of daily routines, such as taking the same bus to work or eating the same cereal for breakfast, helps them insert some predictability into their day. However, an employee's need for routine and sameness at work can extend beyond this, triggering an extreme reaction to changes in surroundings, routine, and people. For example, an employee may be upset by changes to the physical environment, such as a different layout of office furniture or being moved to a different cubicle, or even a different brand of coffee in the breakroom. Personnel changes can also be disruptive, such as when the individual is required to report to a different supervisor, or new co-workers arrive on the scene.

"One of the things that helps me minimize my anxiety with transition is when I'm advised in advance of schedule changes or meetings, when possible. It increases my anxiety significantly when I'm at the last minute asked to do something and that goes out of the scheme that I planned in my head."

Changes in schedules can be problematic as well. Most people can easily adjust to a 15-minute delay in the start of a meeting, using the time to answer email or get another cup of coffee, then leaving the meeting early if there is a scheduling conflict due to the change. However, handling this seemingly small change in one's day is not as easy for an individual on the spectrum. If transitioning from one activity to another is a challenge for the employee (as discussed in Chapter 9), he will now have to face *two more* transitions: shifting to an interim activity, then shifting back to begin the meeting. He also may become anxious if he has scheduled a task to start at a specific time after the meeting, which will now have to be delayed. Most likely he will enter the meeting complaining about the delay, leaving his colleagues to wonder why he is making such a big deal over nothing.

What is it about changes that make them so difficult for an individual on the spectrum to accept? The inflexibility that is typically part of being on the autism spectrum (discussed in Chapter 10) is certainly a factor. However, some experts in autism speculate that resistance to change may be due to the overly detail-oriented way in which people on the spectrum perceive their world (discussed in Chapter 12). As you will recall from previous chapters, people with autism tend to perceive minute details, often at the expense of the "big picture," and they notice differences more readily than similarities. To individuals with autism, if something is not the same, it changes the perception of the whole. The slightest change in a detail, such as a piece of furniture that has been moved a few inches, or a small deviation in a routine, no longer matches the exact concept they have stored from past experience or memory, so they do not know what they are expected to do, which can result in confusion, frustration, and anxiety.[56]

If the change is more involved (e.g. relocation to another work station or a change in the work environment), an employee on the spectrum may be out of sorts for a while, and more susceptible to sensory overload, such as office background noise. They may also struggle with tasks that are normally easy for them, until they make the adjustment. To help an employee cope with the change, address it in advance, providing as much information as you can. He may ask for information that might seem inconsequential to you, but keep in mind that he is most likely trying to reconcile how he will deal with all of the differences he perceives, so work with the employee to focus on what is *not* changing.

Because of his resistance to change, an employee on the spectrum may stubbornly refuse when asked to modify a process or procedure, especially if he thinks the request is arbitrary or random. Keep in mind that he may not understand how his work fits into the "big picture" or how it will be used (see Chapter 10), and he therefore might interpret the change as not relevant or feel that it will lead to errors. Individuals with autism generally respond best to solid evidence or reasoning, so explaining *why* the change is needed will be more effective than saying, "Do it because I asked you to."

For people on the autism spectrum, routines play a major role in establishing control or managing stress when they are anxious or under pressure at work. They might get irritated when their routine is altered, because it means that they must prepare again or relearn something. Although it is generally beneficial to challenge an employee to try new things, change just for the sake of change may not have the intended positive effect if the employee is on the spectrum.

Emotional control

When situations such as changes or interruptions upset or frustrate an individual on the spectrum, he may have difficulty regulating his behavior or controlling his impulses because of challenges with the executive function of *emotional regulation*.

As mentioned in the introduction to this chapter, emotional regulation allows us to control how much emotion we let out, similar to a pressure valve. Individuals with autism, however, tend to have only an "on/off" switch.

> *"People with Asperger's are either a 1 or a 10. When you're angry you're angry, and when you're not, you're not. There's no in-between."*

When the emotional regulation of an individual on the spectrum is weakened, it affects his self-control in general, and may make it difficult to avoid the cumulative effect of small things that grab his emotional attention. Stress, frustration, and anger in reaction to interruptions, a request to change something, or thinking about an incident that took place earlier in the day, can all contribute to the loss of emotional control.

Although people with autism may have the best of intentions to control their behavior and emotional outbursts, doing so takes a great deal of energy. Dealing with the daily challenges they encounter may deplete the energy they need to keep themselves emotionally balanced, so they may succumb to the need to gain momentary relief from frustration and other negative emotions by having an outburst or meltdown.[57]

Difficulties with emotional regulation may also result in an overreaction to others' emotions or a distortion of the magnitude of a situation. An employee on the spectrum may have a tendency to "lose it" when trying to multitask, or when supervisors set contradictory priorities. Sensory overload, such as too noisy an environment (covered in Chapter 13) may also build frustration and cause the employee to become upset.

An individual with autism might not be able to express the growing frustration inside him, but physical changes may signal an imminent emotional outburst:

> *"My face gets very red, my eyes go really round—that's an indication that I need a break, that I need to go somewhere and collect myself. Then I can come back, and we can speak about*

whatever we were speaking about. But you need to give me that time away from the situation."

Sometimes the emotional reaction of an employee may seem to come out of nowhere, leaving colleagues to ask, "What's wrong?" An individual with autism may have difficulty identifying his emotions and even more trouble verbalizing them. He may not be able to discern subtle differences in his emotional state and may interpret high levels of any negative emotion, including anxiety, as anger. Keep in mind that when someone on the spectrum says that he does not know what he is feeling, it is most likely a literal statement.

When an employee on the spectrum gets upset, frustrated or angry, chiding him or commenting that he is making a "big deal out of nothing" or telling him to "calm down" does little to keep him from escalating. Give him time to recoup and reregulate by suggesting he take a brief walk or return to his office. Later, you can calmly discuss the situation and what can be done to prevent it from happening again in the future.

How do you deal with an employee who is bothered by everything?

When dealing with issues related to anxiety, change, or emotional regulation, remember that the negative reaction of an individual with autism may not be under his control. Understanding the most common sources of frustration and anger in the workplace for an employee on the spectrum will go a long way toward lessening the impact or keeping a situation from escalating.

Anxiety is a common issue for people on the spectrum who are constantly struggling to make sense of the way neurotypicals act and think, as well as trying to fit into their world. Issues of work performance (discussed in previous chapters) may be the cause of much anxiety, because employees with autism want to perform well and may fear being given a poor evaluation or being terminated (whether those concerns are warranted or not). As mentioned previously, an employee with autism may become anxious for various reasons:

- not understanding what is expected of him
- not operating as quickly or as efficiently as expected
- receiving demands from multiple people at the same time
- receiving criticism.

An employee with autism may feel anxious, but not understand why. He may not recognize that he is becoming overwhelmed during the early stages, so it is important to intervene if you notice that the person is becoming anxious or agitated. Keep in mind that due to black-and-white thinking, his interpretation of the situation may be out of proportion, so try to determine the source of his anxiety:

- Is the anxiety work-related?
- Is he anxious about how to handle a social situation or upcoming social event?
- Is he worried about controlling his impulses?
- Was he overly affected when someone yelled or exhibited other strong emotions?

Sensory challenges such as being exposed to excessive noise, light, and other sensory inputs (covered in Part Four) can also raise anxiety levels. To avoid an escalation of anxiety, allow an employee on the spectrum temporarily to leave a stressful situation or discussion by taking a walk or a short break so that he can collect himself.

Dealing with *change* of any kind can be challenging, and it is difficult for people on the spectrum to understand that in a work world, things do not flow as expected. For people who are new to the workforce, explain that in your employment environment, change is inevitable; different stakeholders have agendas that may shift at any time, which generally causes disruptions of varying degrees that every employee will have to deal with at some point:

- For schedule changes, give a person on the spectrum advance notice, if possible, and provide guidance on reviewing priorities and adjusting the rest of his schedule accordingly.

- For last-minute meeting changes, provide a list of options the employee can follow, depending on the length of the delay, such as taking a few minutes of down time.

- If there is a more significant change, such as a move to a different workstation or a change in supervisor, help the individual see what will remain the *same*, then explain what might be different and work together to address concerns.

Allow the employee to ask questions about a change and address them, even if they seem trivial—keep in mind that for an individual on the spectrum, the differences in small details may elicit the most anxiety!

When you ask an employee on the spectrum to change the way he has been doing a procedure or process, he might argue or refuse, in an attempt to maintain control over what he anticipates to be anxiety-provoking. Keep in mind that the employee is not trying to be stubborn or contrary. When you request that an employee with autism change the way he has been doing something, he must formulate a plan to "unlearn" the old way and learn the new, which takes a great deal of cognitive energy. Again, stress what will remain the same and explain the change as part of the "big picture" of what it will accomplish.

An employee with autism may lose *emotional control* due to the buildup of frustration or aggravation from constant interruptions and minor changes in routines throughout the day. Give him a chance to cool down before attempting to discuss the situation, and suggest he "Take a 15-minute break" or "Take a walk outside" or go someplace that is calming for him. This will give him the space and time to recoup and reregulate and keep his emotions from escalating.

Most of us have internal mechanisms that allow us to control how much emotion we let out, like a pressure valve, while the emotions of an employee with autism may quickly escalate. You can, however, encourage emotional self-control in the individual by designating a quiet location for a self-imposed "time-out" when needed, enabling him to de-stress and relax without any social expectations or demands placed on him. If there are several things that continually lead to a loss of control, develop a "cheat sheet" with the individual as a reminder that lists each situation along with a positive thought or action he can take to keep his frustration or anxiety in check.

Related material

- Chapter 9: Time Management

- Chapter 10: Work Quality

- Chapter 13: Sensory Overload

Section 11.2: Is this job too much for him?

I guess she's not a fan of birthday parties.

Topics covered

- Withdraws for no apparent reason
- Seems tired by mid-week
- Asks to work off-hours or from home

Are you seeing these behaviors?

- An employee seems tired by mid-week and is asking to work from home... *And you think to yourself, "Is this job too much for him?"*
- One of your employees refuses to attend the department's "volunteer day" activity.

What are the underlying issues?
Face time and social demands of the workplace
For an employee with autism, getting through the workday requires extra effort as he manages the challenges of social interactions, executive functioning, and sensory issues (covered in Part Four), all while trying to do his job well.

Most companies require office presence or "face time," as the work environment depends on harmonious interaction among employees, so they can work together efficiently to meet the goals of the organization. Navigating the rules of the social aspects of the workplace (discussed in Part Two) can be confusing and stressful for many individuals on the autism spectrum, which may leave them exhausted from daily interactions with people at work.

"I become extremely fatigued from interacting with people by mid-work week."

The constant flow of information while completing assignments and working on teams depends on social interaction as well. Those on the spectrum require more alone time than other people to "recharge their batteries," as continually trying to interpret the needs of colleagues and managers can deplete their energy. Some individuals on the spectrum may withdraw from social contact for periods of time as a means of control; having less contact means potentially dealing with less stress. For example, an employee on the spectrum may prefer to eat lunch alone or avoid other social gatherings related to the workplace.

Emotional exhaustion

Some people with autism put in a great deal of effort trying to "appear normal," and attempting to hide behaviors that are a part of the individual's neurological makeup. This is called *cloaking*, and it can be exhausting for the individual. For example, an employee who has been criticized in the past for excessive smiling or an unusual tone of voice may need to monitor himself whenever he is in meetings. Individuals who engage in stress-relieving repetitive movements, such as excessive chair rocking, may work to suppress these behaviors, and end up adding to the stress they feel. Providing a space where an individual with autism can express these behaviors in private or allowing him to take a short break may help him remain more relaxed and productive throughout the day.

"I think that fatigue comes from being intensely focused when I'm at work, and I just run out of energy."

Individuals with autism may become exhausted from many aspects of doing their job, such as focusing intensely on their work or handling frequent interruptions or demands from multiple people at the same time. When dealing with change (covered in the Section 11.1) an employee on the spectrum may be drained by the mental energy necessary to undo prior learning and formulate a new plan, as well as dealing with any anxiety resulting from anticipation of the change.

"I think that one of the things that employers need to be aware of with people with Asperger's in the workplace, is they do have thresholds, and those thresholds can sometimes be very low."

Of course, as with any person, when you are exhausted, it is much more difficult to take control of your emotions. An employee on the spectrum who already has challenges with emotional regulation may find it even more difficult to "keep it together" when he is emotionally depleted, so it is important that he have a way of removing himself from a stressful situation, such as taking a short walk or going to an empty office. Provide scheduled breaks to avoid mental fatigue, including getting up for a drink of water or rotating through varied tasks.

Shutting down and withdrawing

People on the autism spectrum tend to have a hypersensitivity to experiences, when everything in their environment can be overwhelming. As we will discuss in Chapter 13, this is often due to sensitivity to sensory input, such as lights, noises, and smells. Emotional experiences can be intensified as well, leaving the individual feeling overpowered, anxious, and fearful.

As discussed in Section 11.1, *loss of emotional control* is related to difficulty with emotional regulation and is often a response to the buildup of multiple sources of frustration or anxiety over the day, resulting in an outburst or meltdown. *Shutting down*, on the other hand, is a response to being overwhelmed, where the brain shuts down as self-protection before it can become overloaded. When a person on the spectrum shuts down, he experiences it as a brief interlude when his brain stops processing, causing him to "zone out." He may not be able to focus on the conversation and may even look blank, frozen, or confused.

Keep in mind that when an individual on the spectrum shuts down, it is a *physical* response that is not under his control. For example, when the sun is too bright, you close or shade your eyes—to resist shielding them from the sun would be very uncomfortable. When you see an employee shutting down, a natural reaction is to speak more loudly or gesture at the person to get his attention or try to snap him out of it, which generally has little effect. Give him a few minutes to regain his focus.

Inflexible schedules

As mentioned previously, employees on the autism spectrum often need a break from social interaction and the stress of getting through the day-to-day activities of the neuro-typical workplace. Some individuals will find it sufficient to have short breaks throughout the workday, while others may need more concentrated periods of time away from social interaction and interruptions to perform at their highest levels.

Although the corporate world is changing because of globalization, and many companies conduct business across multiple time zones, the mindset of a standardized "9 to 5, Monday to Friday" work environment is still the norm. For employees on the spectrum who get emotionally exhausted from the demands of the workplace, sustaining the level of energy needed to get their work done for five days may wear them down to the point where they are less productive. Additionally, this sustained but emotionally draining effort may make it difficult to stay on an even keel emotionally.

> *"Fridays are very, very difficult days because I'm tired. And being tired doesn't allow you to overcome some of the automatic traits of Asperger's."*

Many companies have found that strategies such as *flextime* and working from home (*telework* or *telecommuting*) contribute greatly to increased productivity—for *all* employees, including employees with autism. This *workplace flexibility* may involve structured breaks, so an employee on the spectrum can recharge his batteries or de-stress. The flexibility can also be applied to the scheduling of work projects, so that there is a minimum of shifting between tasks or interruptions. If prolonged interactions with colleagues is necessary for certain projects, such as team meetings, a manager can schedule a day each week where social interactions are *not* required or are minimal.

> "I have one day where I don't interact with so many people, and it just allows me to alleviate some of the stress associated with that."

Allowing an employee on the spectrum the opportunity to adjust his schedule so that he arrives and leaves earlier or later than his colleagues may help him avoid the social interactions that start and end the day in many workplaces, or the stress of traveling during peak commuting times.

If the employee repeatedly asks to work from home, he may need a break from the physical work environment in general (although not from the work itself), and might benefit from occasionally working from home. For example, a researcher working on complicated or lengthy reports may work from home one day a week to avoid the constant interruptions at work.

While we generally associate workplace flexibility with when and where employees work, it can also refer to flexibility in work assignments. For example, a manager can schedule work for a project so that an individual on the spectrum can complete chunks of it without interruption, or schedule tasks that require extended focus and concentration during the time of day when the employee has the most mental energy.

Keep in mind that although an employee on the spectrum may perform best when there is *flexibility* in the way he does his job, once the accommodation is settled upon, it should be implemented in a *structured* way. For example, if the employee needs one day away from the interruptions of the office, designating a specific day of the week and what work can be completed within that time frame is more effective than merely instructing him to "Take a day off to work at home."

The right person for the right job

Every job has a social component and a work performance component, and addressing the issue in these areas for an employee on the autism spectrum might lead a manager to ask, "Is this the right person for the right job?" In many respects, the answer is no different for someone on the spectrum than it is for someone who is not: are the requirements of this job in alignment with the competency and skills of the individual? An additional consideration (which is the focus of this book) is, "Can the employee's challenges related to the autism spectrum be *reasonably accommodated*?"

Autism truly is a "spectrum" of strengths and challenges of various natures and degrees, so there is no single "profile" that fits all individuals. There are people on the spectrum who are quite outgoing and in many respects effective communicators, and those who work best when limited social interaction is required. There are people on the spectrum who are highly organized and detail-oriented, and those who are not. Others may struggle with the flexibility required for ever-changing schedules, a high amount of team interactions, and shifting project requirements and priorities.

When a manager notices challenges within a particular area that impede the job performance of an employee with autism, a natural reaction is to assume that job is not a good fit, such as a customer service position, where an employee may have to deal with dissatisfied customers or simultaneously listen to customers while logging details of the issue into a computer.

Some people on the spectrum excel in jobs that utilize their technical expertise, but have great difficulty when their role shifts to one of management, where there is generally a greater emphasis placed on interpersonal and executive function skills, seeing the "big picture," and decision-making. Other job aspects that might affect an employee with autism include:

- interacting with people in multiple departments and teams or with clients

- working on multiple projects simultaneously and juggling conflicting agendas

- adjusting to priorities or schedules that constantly shift

- making decisions that might impact other projects or procedures

- working in different locations

- requiring a great deal of "face time" or socializing.

As with all employees, the right job for the individual's expertise is critical to having a successful employment relationship. Employees with autism can be invaluable contributors in all types of jobs; however, it does not benefit the employee or the employer to have someone in a job where they will continue to struggle, no matter what accommodations and management strategies are implemented. That said, sometimes it may be necessary to assess if the employee's challenges related to autism significantly impact his ability to meet the essential requirements of the job, and if so, determine how to deal with it.

If you determine the employee does not meet the essential requirements of the job, take an inventory of the employee's skill set and look elsewhere in your organization for an appropriate position for the employee in question. If no other appropriate position exists, be sure to follow the stated policies and procedures your company has in place for terminating employees, and explain to the employee the gaps in skill sets resulting in your decision.

How do you deal with an employee who seems emotionally drained by his job?

The effort needed for an employee with autism to manage the challenges of social interactions and executive functioning on a daily basis may leave him emotionally exhausted. Not only will this affect the individual's productivity, but it may make it more difficult for him to regulate his emotions. You can give the employee opportunities to "recharge his batteries" in various ways:

- Provide a quiet place for the employee to calm down when he is overloaded.

- Try to limit frequent interruptions or demands from multiple people at the same time.

- Allow the individual to withdraw from social contact when necessary by not insisting he eat lunch with colleagues or attend social gatherings related to the workplace.

- Schedule short breaks throughout the day.

- Limit the amount of required office presence or "face time."

When a person on the spectrum experiences too much overload, he may "shut down" or have a brief interlude when his brain stops processing, making it difficult for him to respond to anything. Shutting down is a physical response that is not under the employee's control, so give him a few minutes to regain his focus.

Allowing an employee with autism the flexibility to adjust how, when, and where he works, when appropriate, can be a very effective accommodation. Any adjustments should be implemented with consistency in mind, so that the individual knows what to expect each day. If an employee is drained by too much social interaction or too many interruptions, allow him to work from home one day each week. Keep the day of the week consistent and outline exactly what work you want him to do. To minimize difficulties transitioning from home to workplace, assign work that can be completed at home in the time frame of a workday. Modifying an employee's start time so that he arrives before his colleagues can help cut down on the amount of exposure to social interaction.

Lastly, as you would with any employee, ensure that employees on the spectrum are in the right job for their skill sets; and do not mistake challenges related to autism as an inability to do the job.

Related material

- Section 11.1

- Chapter 13: Sensory Overload

- Part Two: Social Issues at Work

- Part Four: Sensory Issues at Work

Emotional regulation: Accommodations summary

The ability to control how one expresses emotions is called *emotional regulation*. For individuals on the autism spectrum, emotional regulation may be one of their executive functioning challenges. They may overreact, or become anxious, frustrated, or irritated for what seems to be no apparent reason.

Anxiety is the biggest emotional regulation challenge for most individuals on the spectrum. Having a history of making social missteps, misreading nonverbal cues, misunderstanding priorities, and missing the big picture can understandably make someone nervous and anxious. Add to that the worry about not doing a good job, or being terminated, and an employee on the spectrum often struggles to keep his anxiety in check. Therefore, small deviations in the work environment may cause an employee on the spectrum to lose emotional control, as they are already in a heightened state of stress.

Most work environments place social demands on employees that many of us take for granted—team projects, lunch with co-workers, birthday parties, volunteer days, and holiday parties. Many employees on the spectrum have developed coping mechanisms to get through the social demands of their workplace, but find they are exhausted by these efforts. Some people with autism expend a great deal of effort to "appear normal" by hiding, or *cloaking*, behaviors that are part of their neurological makeup. This too is exhausting, leaving many individuals less able to maintain emotional control throughout the day. As a result, some employees on the spectrum may shut down or withdraw in order to calm themselves and regain their focus.

Employees on the spectrum may be responding to anxiety or emotional regulation issues when exhibiting the following behaviors:

- overreacting to minor incidents

- appearing tired or exhausted

- shutting down or withdrawing.

> Stress consistently shows up in surveys as one of the top ten reasons that employees are absent from work. Strategies to reduce stress in the workplace benefit all employees, reduce employers' costs, and are generally sound management practices.

Reducing anxiety for employees on the autism spectrum affords them a greater chance of maintaining emotional control and performing to the best of their ability. An employee with autism may feel anxious, but not understand why, so try to determine the source of his anxiety:

- Is the anxiety work-related?

- Is he anxious about how to handle a social situation or upcoming social event?

- Is he worried about controlling his impulses?

- Was he overly affected when someone yelled or exhibited other strong emotions?

While individuals on the spectrum will develop their own coping mechanisms, employers can operate in ways that reduce uncertainty and help the individual maintain emotional control, especially if he has difficulty with change.

- Help an employee cope with change by addressing it in advance, providing as much information as you can.

- Explain why changes are necessary, and only make changes to the employee's routine if truly necessary.

- Do not tell an employee on the spectrum he is making a "big deal out of nothing" or to "calm down" to keep him from escalating. Acknowledge his concerns, and then give him time to recoup and reregulate by suggesting he take a brief walk or break. Later, you can calmly discuss the situation and what can be done to prevent it from happening again in the future.

- Ensure a good match between the skill sets of the employee and the requirements of the job.

For employees that seem drained by the social, or "face time", demands of the workplace, making adjustments to allow them time to withdraw and recharge is very effective.

- Provide a quiet place in your office for the employee to take a break when necessary.

- Schedule short breaks for the employee during the day.

- Do not take offense if the individual chooses not to join colleagues for lunch or non-mandatory social activities.

- Allow for a flexible work schedule or time to work from home, if possible. Keep scheduling accommodations structured and consistent to minimize difficulties with transitioning and changes.

As you would with any employee, ensure that employees on the spectrum are in the right job for their skill sets; and do not mistake challenges related to autism as an inability to do the job.

Part Four

SENSORY ISSUES AT WORK

Chapter 12

INTRODUCTION TO SENSORY ISSUES AT WORK

Sensory processing is spontaneous, so we do not give it much thought. We rarely notice all the information that hits our senses, because we pay attention to what is important, given the context of the situation we are in, and generally disregard the rest. For example, if you are in a meeting, when a car honks its horn outside your office window, you will probably barely notice it. On the other hand, if you are at home, waiting for a car service to take you to the airport, hearing a car honk will most likely grab your attention.

The workplace is filled with sensory stimuli: the sounds of printers, copiers, and people talking; office lighting and computer screens; as well as the smells of coffee brewing in the breakroom and a colleague's perfume. Most of these potential sensory distractions fade into the background as you work. An individual on the spectrum, however, may have difficulty filtering out the sensory elements of the workplace and become distracted by them. For example, he may notice the hum or flickering of fluorescent lighting, or may not be able to distinguish the voice of the person speaking to him from the other sounds in the environment. Needless to say, these sensory challenges can be overwhelming and can impact how well he can do his job.

How we perceive the world

According to autism researcher Olga Bogdashina, "the way a person perceives the world affects the way he or she stores and utilizes information."[58] The *neuro-typical* brain coordinates input from a person's senses, filters it based on the context of the situation, then focuses on the relevant information. Cognitive processes such as *theory of mind*, *central coherence* (getting the "big picture") and the *executive functions* then interpret the information according to the context of the situation and past experiences, which in turn influences what the person thinks, how he behaves, and how well he does his job (see Figure 12.1).

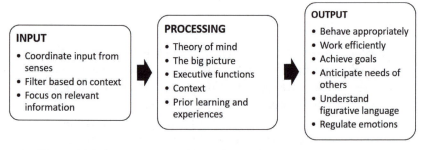

Figure 12.1: Sensory perception and cognitive processes

For example, when an employee hears a request for information from his manager, he focuses on *what she is saying* and the *tone of her voice* (tuning out the rest of the office sounds), as well as her *facial expression* (rather than what she is wearing). He understands (via *theory of mind*) that his manager considers the request urgent, and gets her the information as quickly as possible.

Sensory issues and autism

Although a person on the autism spectrum may receive the same sensory input as a neuro-typical colleague, *how* he processes it may be vastly different. Without the means for filtering sensory information, the sounds, lights, and smells of the workplace may be distracting or he may become overwhelmed by them.

Sensory sensitivities are part of the criteria used to diagnose an autism spectrum disorder,[59] although they can vary in type and severity from individual to individual. The sensitivity to sensory input is neurologically based, and while individuals on the spectrum may learn to be less sensitive to certain sensory stimuli over time, their reactions are generally not under their control.

How an individual with autism processes sensory information may affect many other cognitive processes. For example, he may not be able to determine which details are important, affecting his ability to grasp the gist of a situation. He may restrict his attention to only one channel of input, such as avoiding eye contact while listening to someone's voice, or he may focus intently on details that are irrelevant.

Sensory perception that is incomplete, missing, or compromised can negatively impact some of the cognitive processes of an individual on the spectrum, which may result in inappropriate social behavior, and difficulties with job performance and emotional control (see Figure 12.2). When sensory input is overwhelming, it can lead to sensory overload.

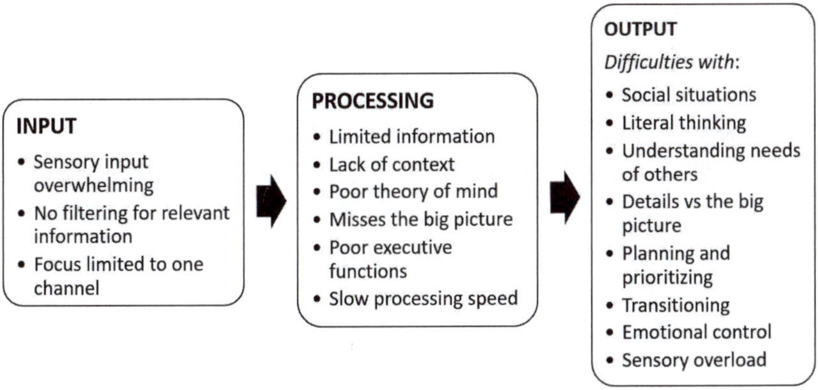

INPUT
- Sensory input overwhelming
- No filtering for relevant information
- Focus limited to one channel

PROCESSING
- Limited information
- Lack of context
- Poor theory of mind
- Misses the big picture
- Poor executive functions
- Slow processing speed

OUTPUT
Difficulties with:
- Social situations
- Literal thinking
- Understanding needs of others
- Details vs the big picture
- Planning and prioritizing
- Transitioning
- Emotional control
- Sensory overload

Figure 12.2: Effect of sensory perception problems

Typical sensory challenges at work

An employee on the autism spectrum with sensory issues may:

- have a sensitivity to fluorescent or harsh lighting
- find typical office sounds (e.g. printers, copiers, and people talking) very distracting
- complain about smells (e.g. food, perfume, and other typical office odors)
- exhibit unusual repetitive behaviors when stressed
- prefer to sit in the dark or wear headphones all the time
- become overwhelmed by the social commotion in the office.

Disclosure and accommodations for sensory issues

Sensory issues are distracting and enervating, and many individuals with an autism spectrum diagnosis are aware of their sensory challenges and what accommodations they need to work without distraction and perform at their fullest. However, it is important that managers have an *understanding* of the ways sensory issues may affect an individual on the spectrum, and how the employee may react to them. Accommodations are, for the most part, easy to make, and include ways to modify the work environment so that it is *autism-friendly* and helps the employee cope with sensory sensitivities (see Table 12.1).

Table 12.1: Accommodations for sensory issues

	Definition	Example
Understanding	Ways of looking at sensory issues from the perspective of people on the spectrum	People on the spectrum are often distracted by the humming or flickering of fluorescent lights.
Strategies	Simple tactics that you can use	Allow an individual to wear noise-canceling headphones or replace fluorescent bulbs with incandescent bulbs.

In the next chapter, *Sensory Overload*, we will discuss the most common behaviors related to sensory issues and various accommodations to deal with them effectively.

Chapter 13

SENSORY OVERLOAD

As discussed in Chapter 12, the five senses work together to filter stimuli coming from the environment, which the brain then interprets. Generally, you are not aware of all the sensory information surrounding you, because your brain's screening system enables you to pay attention only to what is most important and relevant at any given moment, based on the *context* of a situation. For example, if you are having a conversation on a busy street, you tend to focus on the other person's voice and pay less attention to the sounds of traffic, passersby, and other street noises. An individual on the spectrum, however, may not be able to *filter* out the sound of someone's voice from other extraneous noises that his brain receives and will have difficulty concentrating on what the other person is saying. It may be particularly difficult when someone with autism tries to juggle *two sensory* inputs, such as the visual information obtained by looking someone in the eye and the auditory information received while listening to him; they can focus on one or the other, but not both simultaneously, which results in their typical lack of eye contact during conversations, as discussed in Chapter 6.

The sights, noises, and smells of a busy workplace represent a wide range of sensory stimuli that the brain needs to process, paying attention to the most important, based on the context of the situation. Individuals with autism, however, process input to their senses differently, and may experience these sensations with equal intensity. This often leads to *sensory overload*, making it difficult for them to focus on the task at hand. Sensitivity to the visual, auditory, and olfactory stimuli that most people ignore can become a constant interruption for an employee on the spectrum, causing him to have to constantly shift his attention back to what he is doing.

The most common sensory issues for individuals with autism include:

- sensitivity to fluorescent or bright lights

- low tolerance for certain noises

- extreme reactions to perfumes or smells.

In this chapter, we will cover the most common ways the sensory aspect of the workplace affects employees on the autism spectrum, and the adaptive behaviors that they use to counter sensory overload. We will also address the simple accommodations that can make the work environment *autism-friendly*.

On a positive note:

- Challenges related to sensory issues are easily accommodated.

- Most individuals on the spectrum are very conscious of their sensory sensitivities and have developed coping mechanisms that enable them to work productively.

As you read this chapter, please remember that not all individuals with autism will display all the behaviors discussed. Each individual on the spectrum is different, and their challenges related to autism will be unique to them.

Section 13.1: What is his problem?

SENSORY OVERLOAD

Topics covered

- Complains about lighting or sits in the dark
- Insists on wearing headphones while working
- Annoyed by typical office noises
- Complains about every smell
- Dislikes being touched
- Wants a non-standard workspace

Are you seeing these behaviors?

- An employee constantly complains about the copier noise and asks to be moved... *And you think to yourself, "What is his problem?"*
- When a co-worker eats at the desk, an employee next tells them how badly their food smells.

What are the underlying issues?

The typical open office environment that is designed to be more conducive to collaboration and communication can be an assault on our senses, yet we take for granted our capacity to filter out background noise and other possible distractions. Many people with autism, however, do not have this ability, and they can easily become distracted and overwhelmed by the sensory aspects of the workplace. These *sensory sensitivities* may add to the anxiety of employees on the spectrum, especially when they are in combination with the pressure of dealing with the social and work performance challenges discussed in previous chapters.

People with autism may experience sensory difficulties as *interruptions*, so dealing with sensory issues may take its toll on their work performance. On the other hand, effective work performance strategies that minimize stress, such as providing structure and routine, and giving advance warning of change, may help the employee cope better with sensory situations.[60]

Sensory sensitivities must be addressed, so that employees on the spectrum can be effective in their work. Managers need to be aware of how employees on the spectrum *experience* sensory sensitivities, understand how these difficulties *affect* them, and *accommodate* accordingly. These accommodations may involve modifying the work environment to minimize sensory overload or providing the employee with ways to reduce exposure to the sensory aspects of the office that affect him.

Office lighting

> *"Fluorescent lights are pretty tough on my eyes, so I try not to use them and use a desk lamp."*

Most likely you do not pay much attention to the fluorescent lights in your office, except to notice that they are on or off. People with auditory and visual sensitivities, such as individuals on the autism spectrum, may actually hear the "hum" of fluorescent lights and notice the flickering, that most people do not see. This can be hard on their eyes and very distracting, but lighting issues can easily be addressed.

Replacing fluorescent lights with an incandescent desk lamp deals with both auditory and visual sensitivities. Allowing an employee to wear a baseball cap or visor to block out the light can be sufficient for those affected only by the flickering. Relocating the employee to a workspace near a natural light source may reduce the need for overhead lighting in general during daylight hours.

Office noises

"Everything from the ventilation system when the air conditioning kicks in, to people's footsteps to pens dropping on a desk, keyboards going, chatter, things like that, will keep me from being able to fully concentrate."

Busy offices are a cacophony of sounds with phones ringing, faxes beeping, keyboards clattering, copiers whirring, and people chattering. When most people are concentrating on the task at hand, these noises recede into the background. People on the autism spectrum, however, often find it impossible to filter them out, making it difficult for them to concentrate on their work.

Even quiet sounds may be painful and annoying, such as the hum from fluorescent lights mentioned previously, or the noise from printers, copiers, and other equipment. An employee with sensitivity to office noises may become cranky, and his reaction may be intensified if he is already stressed or anxious.

If it is not possible to move the person to a quieter area of the office, there are several methods of blocking out distracting sounds:

- "Noise-canceling" headphones filter background noises while still allowing the employee to hear normal conversation.

- An MP3 player with ear buds allows the employee to mask background noise by listening to music.

- Some "open" offices have installed sound-masking systems that soften office noises and speech so they are less distracting. "White noise" machines that emit an indistinct sound to mask background noises may have the opposite effect, as some individuals on the spectrum find that the constant background sound is like a roaring in their ears.

- A noise-reducing screen or partition can be used to provide a quiet corner in a noisy office, and carpets, curtains, and soft furnishings can further muffle some office sounds.

Many individuals with autism are not able to pay attention to more than one sound at a time, so it is best to hold work-related conversations in a quiet office, so the employee can more easily focus on your voice. Noisy social situations may be uncomfortable and exhausting for an employee on the spectrum, so allow the individual to step outside or leave if necessary.

Office smells

Some individuals with autism are very sensitive to smells and may be overwhelmed by the scents of perfumes, deodorants, food, and cleaning products. To address sensitivities to smells:

- Use fragrance-free cleaning products.

- Replace scented soaps, hand lotions, and room deodorizers in the restrooms with fragrance-free versions.

- Use an air purifier or small desk fan to reduce the effect of some odors.

Conversely, an employee on the autism spectrum may not be aware of personal hygiene issues such as their own body odor. Directly discuss the situation with the employee and offer suggestions such as fragrance-free deodorants, or more frequent showers or clothing changes.

Clothing and touch

When you get dressed in the morning, you feel your clothes on your skin for a few seconds, but then your body gets used to it. Because of the process of *habituation*, the feeling fades, and you are no longer aware of the clothes you are wearing, until you change them and put on something else. For many people with autism, however, the habituation process does not work properly. This results in an over-sensitivity to clothing on the skin, so they may take off shoes, ties, and jackets at every opportunity. In a work environment where employees on the spectrum must adhere to a dress code, this sensory aspect can be very challenging.

An employee may be sensitive to certain fabrics, or restrictive clothing in general. If your workplace has a strict dress code that dictates formal office wear, allow the employee to wear a formal shirt without the tie or wear comfortable shoes in his office. Feeling uncomfortable in work clothing may eventually make an individual on the spectrum stressed and anxious throughout the entire day, and he may not realize why he is feeling that way.

Some people on the spectrum have sensitivity to touch and may avoid shaking hands, and a light pat on the shoulder may be uncomfortable.

People with autism sometimes have strong food preferences and aversions. They may only like a restricted list of foods, or foods that are a certain color or texture. If an employee needs to eat in a work-related situation, a manager should treat it as he would an allergy or any other food-based issue.

How do you deal with an employee who is bothered by the office environment?

Managers need to be aware of any sensory problems experienced by an employee on the spectrum. It is important to understand how these issues may affect the individual physically and emotionally, as well as any impact they may have on his work performance. Sensory issues can be addressed through simple changes in the physical work environment, which can minimize sensory overload and make it autism-friendly in general, or by personal accommodations for a specific individual.

Office lighting:

- Replace fluorescent lights with an incandescent desk lamp.

- Allow the employee to wear a baseball cap or visor.

- Relocate the employee to a workspace near a natural light source.

Office noise:

- Allow the employee to wear a noise-canceling headset.

- Mask background noise by allowing the employee to use an MP3 player with ear buds to listen to music.

- Move the person to a quieter area of the office or use a noise-reduction screen or partition.

- Use carpets, curtains, and soft furnishings to muffle office sounds.

- Install a sound-masking system that softens offices noises and speech.

- Hold work-related conversations in a quiet office and allow the employee to leave a noisy social situation if he is uncomfortable.

Office smells:

- Replace cleaning products and restroom toiletries with fragrance-free versions.

- Use an air purifier or small desk fan to reduce the effect of some odors.

If your workplace has a strict dress code that dictates formal office wear, allow the employee to wear a formal shirt without the tie or wear comfortable shoes in his office.

If an employee needs to eat in a work-related situation, a manager should treat it as he would an allergy or any other food-based issue.

Related material

- Chapter 6: Social Interaction

Section 13.2: What is he doing?

Topics covered

- Seems to zone out for no reason

- Fidgets or rocks in meetings

- Exhibits odd, repetitive physical behavior

Are you seeing these behaviors?

- During meetings, a team member is constantly rocking in his chair... *And you think to yourself, "What is he doing?"*

- An employee periodically disappears into an empty office for no apparent reason.

What are the underlying issues?
Dealing with sensory overload

> *"Sometimes when there are too many sensory inputs, your brain will go into reset or pause mode. And it takes a moment for your brain to catch up to everything that's going on around you... It's not anything that's controllable, it's just something that you have to be patient and wait for."*

Too many voices, noises, lights, and other sensory stimuli can become overwhelming to someone with autism. As mentioned in the previous chapter, *sensory overload* occurs when a person experiences too much sensory stimulation at the same time and cannot handle it all, like a fuse that breaks the electrical circuit to avoid a fire when too much power surges through a house's electrical system. Individuals on the spectrum often describe this sensory "shutdown" as a brief interlude when their brain stops processing, causing them to "zone out," making it difficult to continue a conversation; to another person he may appear frozen or confused, or to have a blank look.

Sensory overload or "shutting down," is a *physical* response that is not under his control, just as a person's heart races and adrenaline pumps when danger is sensed. When an employee with autism shuts down because of sensory overload, a natural reaction is to speak more loudly or gesture at the person to get his attention. However, there is really no way that he can voluntarily "snap out of it," and he will need a few minutes free from sensory stimulation or interaction to regain his focus.

An individual on the spectrum may experience sensory overload in a social situation, where trying to process loud music and party lighting while filtering many different people's voices can quickly become overwhelming. If an individual seems anxious or uncomfortable, his system may need a rest to keep from shutting down, so let him leave the room or take him to a quieter place. Just the thought of a loud social gathering may make an individual with autism anxious, so do not force him to attend if he asks to be excused.

An employee with autism may become overwhelmed by sensory stimuli in work situations where he must process more than one person talking. For example, in group meetings, he may experience too much stimulation from being around so many people for an extended period, and the individual may develop a blank look or leave the room several times in order to calm himself. Allow him to take a break when needed, such as going to the restroom or another quiet place for five minutes.

Sometimes an employee on the spectrum may stay in an over-stimulating situation longer than he should, because he feels he will be criticized for leaving the room, which only makes things worse. He may not realize that he is becoming overwhelmed, so if you notice that he is becoming anxious or stressed, intervene and suggest he take a short break.

Self-calming and repetitive behaviors

"Often, I would be rocking back and forth on a chair and not realize that I was doing it, until somebody grabbed my chair and told me to stop."

At times, we all respond to anxiety or stress by engaging in repetitive behaviors such as pacing, tapping fingers on a table, clicking a pen, or bouncing a leg. Researchers at Tel Aviv University found that repetitive behavior in general induces calm and helps manage stress, particularly when faced with unpredictable or uncontrollable events, such as a professional basketball player who bounces the ball exactly six times before attempting a free throw.[61]

Individuals with autism often use repetitive motions (also referred to as self-stimulation or *stimming*) as a means of regulating sensory overload or calming themselves when anxious. Typical self-calming behaviors include rocking movements, fidgeting, making repetitive noises, or engaging in small movements that may be barely noticeable to those around them. Stimming may also include the repetitive use of an object, such as twirling a piece of string or flicking a rubber band.

Repetitive behaviors serve different functions for people on the autism spectrum: for some they can be calming, for others they can be alerting, helping the individual stay on task. They may also be a sign of joy or contentment, signaling that something has occurred that is extremely positive, such as flapping of the arms or hands. Some individuals with autism feel the need to "cloak" or mask some of their stimming behaviors. For example, those who are hand flappers know that flapping their hands in a meeting or during conversation may make others uncomfortable, so they will try to disguise the behavior by sitting on their hands or making it look as if they are stretching.

Keep in mind that repetitive and self-calming behavior serves as a regulating mechanism and is difficult for a person with autism to control; telling the employee to stop may result in his engaging in a *different* repetitive behavior. When stimming or self-calming behavior gets to a point where it is distracting to other people, prompt the individual to take a two-minute break and go to the restroom, then come back.

How do you deal with an employee when his senses get overloaded?

The most important accommodation for helping individuals on the spectrum with sensory overload is *understanding* that it is a *physical* response and out of a person's control. A workplace environment that is *autism-friendly*, as described in Section 13.1, will help reduce the buildup of sensory stimulation that can lead to sensory overload or a sensory shutdown.

For sensory overload situations, allow the employee to remove himself for a few minutes by taking a short break in a quiet place. When an individual on the spectrum *shuts down*, he may not be able to speak, so do not try to "snap him out of it" by talking louder or waving your hands. Calmly give him a few minutes to reset himself. If an employee gets anxious from being in a meeting where many people are talking, let him take a short break and then return.

Social gatherings with many people tend to be very noisy, so an employee may decline or ask to be excused. If he is required to attend for business purposes, help him find a quiet place to take short breaks and allow him to leave if he starts to feel overwhelmed.

If self-calming or repetitive behaviors of an individual on the spectrum are a distraction to others, provide an area where he can do them in private.

Related material

- Section 13.1

- Chapter 6: Social Interaction

Sensory overload: Accommodations summary

Our daily world is full of sensory input. Yet most of us rarely notice all the information that hits our senses, because we pay attention to what is important, given the context, and block out the rest. The workplace is filled with sensory stimuli: the sounds of printers, copiers, and people talking; office lighting and computer screens; as well as the smells of coffee brewing in the breakroom and a colleague's perfume. For an individual on the spectrum, filtering out the sensory elements of the workplace can be exceptionally difficult and distracting. The impact of these sensory challenges can be overwhelming and impact how well an employee can do his job.

If you see employees engaging in the following behaviors, they may be trying to avoid sensory overload or calming themselves in the event of sensory overload:

- sitting in the dark

- wearing a baseball cap

- wearing earbuds

- complaining constantly about noise, lighting, or smells

- taking frequent breaks

- engaging in small repetitive behaviors.

In many ways, sensory issues are the easiest challenges for employers and employees to address in the workplace. The accommodations to create an *autism-friendly* environment, from a sensory perspective, are easy and cheap; and most individuals on the spectrum are aware of their sensory challenges, if any, and know what needs to be done to manage them.

Understanding that an employee with autism may be reacting to their environment in a way that other employees do not, and working with them to remove distractions, will allow them to avoid sensory overload and perform as expected.

Lighting:

- Replace fluorescent lights with incandescent bulbs.

- Allow the employee to wear a baseball cap or visor to block out offending lights.

- Seat the employ near a natural light source.

Noise:

- Hold important work-related conversations in quiet spaces.

- Allow the employee to wear ear buds or a noise-canceling headset.

- Move the person to a quieter part of the office.

- Use sound-absorbing materials in your office design.

- Install a sound-masking system or use white noise machines to mask office noises.

Smell:

- Use fragrance-free products/cleaning supplies.

- Allow the employee to use a small air purifier.

- Have rules about strong perfumes in the office.

- Sit the employee far away from the office breakroom/pantry.

It is important to understand that the reaction an employee on the spectrum may have to certain sensory inputs is a physical one that is out of their control, and it will not always be possible to avoid all situations where sensory overload may occur. When individuals on the spectrum become overwhelmed due to sensory input, understand that they may need to withdraw to calm themselves and regain focus.

- Do not gesture at the person or shout at them to gain their attention.

- Give the person a few minutes of time, free of the sensory stimulation that caused them to become overwhelmed.

- Allow the individual to leave early if it is a social situation that has caused the sensory overload.

- Provide the individual with a private space if engaging in self-calming or repetitive behaviors becomes a distraction to others.

EPILOGUE

THE SPECTRUM OF AUTISM

This book has provided you with the opportunity to learn about the impact autism/Asperger Syndrome has on individuals in the workplace. As you have read, the impacts can be in three main areas—social interaction, work performance, and sensory issues, with a multitude of variations in each. If you read at least two or more of the chapters in this book, you may have noticed that each chapter contains the following highlighted note:

> As you read this chapter, please remember that not all individuals with autism will display all the behaviors discussed. Each individual on the spectrum is different, and their challenges related to autism will be unique to them.

A popular quote in the autism community, attributed to Dr. Stephen Shore, is: "If you've met one person with autism, you've met one person with autism." This statement couldn't be truer. Just as we perceive color as a *spectrum*—where mixing relative amounts of basic colors can yield limitless variations—*autism too, is a spectrum*. The varying degrees of challenges in social interactions, work performance, and sensory issues interact to result in the uniqueness of an individual on the autism spectrum.

The "Big Picture"
Executive Functioning
Processing Speed
Hidden Curriculum
Sensory Issues
Hyperfocus
Theory of Mind

The autism spectrum

As you work with employees on the spectrum, keep in mind that accommodations and management strategies are not "one size fits all"; to be effective they must reflect the individuality of each person. Understanding the *perspective* of people with autism, what it is like to "stand in their shoes," is an all-important part of the accommodation process as well.

While your initial goal in reading this book may have been to receive guidance on a specific issue related to working with or managing an employee with autism, we hope you found a deeper understanding of and appreciation for the uniqueness of your colleagues on the spectrum. We believe it is summed up best by the well-known autism researcher and writer Dr. Brenda Smith Myles:

> Individuals with autism, Asperger's syndrome and social cognitive challenges have limitless potential that can make a work environment a better and more productive environment for all.[62]

REFERENCES

A conversation with Temple Grandin (2006). Accessed 1/28/2017 at www.npr. org/templates/story/story.php?storyId=5165123

A.J. Drexel Autism Institute. (2015). *National Autism Indicators Report.* Accessed 1/28/2017 at http://drexel.edu/autisminstitute/research-projects/research/ ResearchPrograminLifeCourseOutcomes/indicatorsreport/#sthash. IGKi2lUe.dpbs

Allen, D.G. (2008) *Retaining Talent: A Guide to Analyzing and Managing Employee Turnover.* Alexandria, VA: SHRM Foundation.

American Friends of Tel Aviv University (2011). Finding relief in ritual: A healthy dose of repetitive behavior reduces anxiety, says researcher. *Science Daily.* Accessed 1/28/2017 at www.sciencedaily.com/ releases/2011/09/110922093324.htm

Asperger's in the workplace study reveals befits and challenges for managers (2016). *Nottingham Trent University.* Accessed 1/28/2017 at www4.ntu. ac.uk/apps/news/187900-15/Aspergers_in_the_workplace_study_reveals_ benefits_and_challenges_for_mana.aspx

Autism Speaks (2012). Early intervention for toddlers with autism highly effective, study finds. Accessed 1/28/2017 at www.autismspeaks.org/about-us/press-releases/early-intervention-toddlers-autism-highly-effective-study-finds

Baez, S., Rattazzi, A., Gonzalez-Gadea, M.L., Torralva, T., *et al.* (2012). Integrating intention and context: Assessing social cognition in adults with Asperger syndrome. *Frontiers in Human Neuroscience 6.* doi:10.3389/ fnhum.2012.00302

Bancroft, K., Batten, A., Lambert, S., and Madders, T. (2012). *The Way We Are: Autism in 2012.* London: National Autistic Society. Accessed 1/28/2017 at www.autism.org.uk/~/media/20F5BD5ADBDE42479F126C3E550CE5B0. ashx

Best, C., Arora, S., Porter, F., and Doherty, M. (2015). The relationship between subthreshold autistic traits, ambiguous figure perception and divergent thinking. *Journal of Autism and Developmental Disorders 45,* 12, 4064–4073. doi:10.1007/s10803-015-2518-2

Blades, S. (2016). Spotlight on leadership: The multitasking mirage [Podcast]. *HRS Communications, University of Florida.* Accessed 1/28/2017 at http:// news.hr.ufl.edu/2016/02/spotlight-on-leadership-the-multitasking-mirage

Bogdashina, O. (2016). *Sensory Perceptual Issues in Autism and Asperger Syndrome: Different Sensory Experiences – Different Perceptual Worlds* (2nd edn). London: Jessica Kingsley Publishers.

Bradberry, T. (2014). Multitasking damages your brain and career, new studies suggest. *Forbes.* Accessed 1/28/2017 at www.forbes.com/sites/travisbradberry/2014/10/08/multitasking-damages-your-brain-and-career-new-studies-suggest/#634975892c16

Burack, J.A. (2001). *The Development of Autism: Perspectives from Theory and Research.* Mahwah, NJ: Lawrence Erlbaum Associates.

Centers for Disease Control and Prevention (2016a). *Autism spectrum disorder (ASD): Data & statistics.* Accessed 1/28/2017 at www.cdc.gov/ncbddd/autism/data.html

Centers for Disease Control and Prevention (2016b). *Autism spectrum disorder (ASD): Diagnostic criteria.* Accessed 1/28/2017 at www.cdc.gov/ncbddd/autism/hcp-dsm.html

Cone Communications (2013). 2013 Cone Communications Social Impact Study. Accessed 1/28/2017 at www.conecomm.com/research-blog/2013-cone-communications-social-impact-study

Csikszentmihalyi, M. (1990). *Flow: The Psychology of Optimal Experience.* New York, NY: Harper & Row.

Cultural etiquette around the world (2016). *eDiplomat.* Accessed 1/28/2017 at www.ediplomat.com/np/cultural_etiquette/cultural_etiquette.htm

Ewbank, M., Pell, P., Powell, T., von dem Hagen, E., Baron-Cohen, S., and Calder, A. (2015). Reduced repetition suppression to faces in the fusiform face area of adults with autism spectrum conditions. *Journal of Vision 15*, 12, 1210. doi:10.1167/15.12.1210

Florentine, S. (2015). How SAP is hiring autistic adults for tech jobs. *CIO.* Accessed 1/28/2017 at www.cio.com/article/3013221/careers-staffing/how-sap-is-hiring-autistic-adults-for-tech-jobs.html

Gallup Inc. (2006). Too many interruptions at work? *Gallup.* Accessed 1/28/2017 at www.gallup.com/businessjournal/23146/Too-Many-Interruptions-Work.aspx

Geller, L. (2005, Summer). Emotional regulation and autism spectrum. *Autism Spectrum Quarterly*, 14–17. Accessed 1/28/2017 at http://aspergercenter.com/articles/Emotional-Regulation-and-Autism-Spectrum.pdf

Goldstein, S. and Naglieri, J.A. (2013). *Interventions for Autism Spectrum Disorders: Translating Science into Practice.* New York: Springer.

Goleman, D.P. (2006). *Social Intelligence: The New Science of Human Relationships.* New York, NY: Random House.

Grandin, T. (2006). *Thinking in Pictures: And Other Reports from My Life with Autism* (2nd edn). New York, NY: Knopf Doubleday.

Grandin, T. (2009). How does visual thinking work in the mind of a person with autism? A personal account. *Philosophical Transactions of the Royal Society B: Biological Sciences 364*(1522), 1437–1442. doi:10.1098/rstb.2008.0297

Grandin, T. (2010). The need to be perfect. *Autism Asperger's Digest.* Accessed 1/28/2017 at http://autismdigest.com/the-need-to-be-perfect

Hadjikhani, N., Zürcher, N.R., Rogier, O., Hippolyte, L., *et al.* (2014). Emotional contagion for pain is intact in autism spectrum disorders. *Translational Psychiatry 4*, 1, e343. doi:10.1038/tp.2013.113

Happé, F. and Frith, U. (2006). The weak coherence account: Detail-focused cognitive style in autism spectrum disorders. *Journal of Autism and Developmental Disorders 36*, 1, 5–25. doi:10.1007/s10803-005-0039-0

Jarrett, C. (2016). Why it's hard to talk and make eye contact at the same time. *British Psychological Society Research Digest.* Accessed 1/28/2017 at https://digest.bps.org.uk/2016/11/18/why-its-hard-to-talk-and-make-eye-contact-at-the-same-time

Kennedy, P. (2012). Who made that emoticon? *New York Times.* Accessed 1/28/2017 at www.nytimes.com/2012/11/25/magazine/who-made-that-emoticon.html

Kessler Foundation/National Organization on Disability (2010). *Survey of Employment of Americans with Disabilities.* Accessed 1/28/2017 at www.nod.org/downloads/best-practices/06d_2010_employment_survey_final_report.pdf

Kimhi, Y. (2014). Theory of mind abilities and deficits in autism spectrum disorders. *Topics in Language Disorders 34*, 4, 329–343. doi:10.1097/tld.0000000000000033

Kross, E., Bruehlman-Senecal, E., Park, J., Burson, A., *et al.* (2014). Self-talk as a regulatory mechanism: How you do it matters. *Journal of Personality and Social Psychology 106*, 2, 304–324. doi:10.1037/a0035173

Lewis, K.R. (2014). The next frontier in diversity: Brain differences. *Fortune.* Accessed 1/28/2017 at http://fortune.com/2014/12/16/brain-differences-autism-workplace-diversity

Lewis, M. (2010). Betting on the blind side. *Vanity Fair.* Accessed 1/28/2017 at www.vanityfair.com/news/2010/04/wall-street-excerpt-201004

Lorenz, T. and Heinitz, K. (2014). Aspergers—different, not less: Occupational strengths and job interests of individuals with Asperger's syndrome. *PLoS ONE 9*, 6. doi: 10.1371/journal.pone.0100358

Ludlow, A. (n.d.). Sensory issues in the workplace [Interview]. *Asperger Management.* Accessed 1/28/2017 at www.aspergermanagement.com/features-2/sensory-issues-in-the-workplace

Markram, H., Rinaldi, T., and Markram, K. (2007). The intense world syndrome—an alternative hypothesis for autism. *Frontiers in Neuroscience 1*, 1, 77–96. doi:10.3389/neuro.01.1.1.006.2007

McFarland, M. (2015). Why shades of Asperger's syndrome are the secret to building a great tech company. *Washington Post.* Accessed 1/28/2017 at www.washingtonpost.com/news/innovations/wp/2015/04/03/why-shades-of-aspergers-syndrome-are-the-secret-to-building-a-great-tech-company/?utm_term=.2bf9015a526a

Myles, B.S. (2012). Interview. *Asperger's in the Workplace: A Guide for Managers.* New York: Asperger Syndrome Training and Employment Partnership [DVD]. Available from Integrate Autism Employment Advisors, Inc. www.integrateadvisors.org

Myles, B.S., Trautman, M.L., and Schelvan, R.L. (2004). *The Hidden Curriculum: Practical Solutions for Understanding Unstated Rules in Social Situations for Adolescents and Young Adults.* Shawnee Mission, KS: Autism Asperger Publishing.

Navarro, J. (2009). The body language of the eyes. *Psychology Today*. Accessed 1/28/2017 at www.psychologytoday.com/blog/spycatcher/200912/the-body-language-the-eyes

Public Library of Science (2011). Level and nature of autistic intelligence: What about Asperger syndrome? *Science Daily*. Accessed 1/28/2017 at www.sciencedaily.com/releases/2011/09/110928180405.htm

Rogers, K., Dziobek, I., Hassenstab, J., Wolf, O.T., and Convit, A. (2006). Who cares? Revisiting empathy in Asperger syndrome. *Journal of Autism and Developmental Disorders 37*, 4, 709–715. doi:10.1007/s10803-006-0197-8

Shattuck, P.T., Narendorf, S.C., Cooper, B., Sterzing, P.R., Wagner, M., and Taylor, J.L. (2012). Postsecondary education and employment among youth with an autism spectrum disorder. *Pediatrics 129*, 6, 1042–1049. Accessed 1/28/2017 at http://pediatrics.aappublications.org/content/129/6/1042

Shellenbarger, S. (2016). Why you should never tell someone to relax. *Wall Street Journal*. Accessed 1/28/2017 at www.wsj.com/articles/why-you-should-never-tell-someone-to-relax-1471370408

Singh, M. (2015). Young adults with autism more likely to be unemployed, isolated. *NPR*. Accessed 1/28/2017 at www.npr.org/sections/health-shots/2015/04/21/401243060/young-adults-with-autism-more-likely-to-be-unemployed-isolated

Sole-Smith, V. (2015). The history of autism. *Parents*. Accessed 1/28/2017 at www.parents.com/health/autism/history-of-autism

Trotman, A. (2014). Facebook's Mark Zuckerberg: Why I wear the same t-shirt every day. *The Telegraph*. Accessed 1/28/2017 at www.telegraph.co.uk/technology/facebook/11217273/Facebooks-Mark-Zuckerberg-Why-I-wear-the-same-T-shirt-every-day.html

U.S. Department of Labor (2013). *Office of Federal Contract Compliance Programs: Regulations implementing Section 503 of the Rehabilitation Act*. Accessed 1/28/2017 at www.dol.gov/ofccp/regs/compliance/section503.htm

Vermeulen, P. (2012). *Autism as Context Blindness*. Shawnee Mission, KS: Autism Asperger Publishing.

Vermeulen, P. (2014). Context blindness in autism spectrum disorder: Not using the forest to see the trees as trees. *Focus on Autism and Other Developmental Disabilities 30*, 3, 182–192. doi:10.1177/1088357614528799

von Schrader, S., Malzer, V., and Bruyère, S. (2013). Perspectives on disability disclosure: The importance of employer practices and workplace climate. *Employee Responsibilities and Rights Journal 26*, 4, 237–255. doi:10.1007/s10672-013-9227-9

Zell, E., Warriner, A.B., and Albarracín, D. (2012). Splitting of the mind: When the you I talk to is me and needs commands. *Social Psychological and Personality Science, 3*, 5, 549–555. doi:10.1177/1948550611430164

NOTES

1. Singh 2015.
2. Shattuck *et al.* 2012.
3. A.J. Drexel Autism Institute 2015.
4. Sole-Smith 2015.
5. Centers for Disease Control and Prevention 2016a.
6. Autism Speaks 2012.
7. Allen 2008, p.3.
8. Kessler Foundation/National Organization on Disability 2010.
9. Cone Communications 2013.
10. U.S. Department of Labor—OFCCP 2013.
11. Bancroft *et al.* 2012.
12. K.R. Lewis 2014.
13. Florentine 2015.
14. M. Lewis 2010.
15. von Schrader, Malzer, and Bruyère 2013.
16. Myles, Trautman, and Schelvan 2004.
17. Vermeulen 2014.
18. Vermeulen 2012.
19. Burack 2001.
20. Kimhi 2014.
21. Baez *et al.* 2012.
22. Shellenbarger 2016.
23. Rogers *et al.* 2006.
24. Hadjikhani *et al.* 2014.
25. Markram, Rinaldi, and Markram 2007.
26. Jarrett 2016.
27. Navarro 2009.
28. Ewbank *et al.* 2015.
29. Grandin 2010.
30. Goleman 2006, p.85.
31. Pass a project or problem to another person or department without consulting with them first.
32. Put forth a significant amount of time, energy, effort, or intensity into some task or action.
33. Kennedy 2012.

34. Grandin 2006, p.156.
35. "Asperger's in the workplace study reveals benefits and challenges for managers" 2016.
36. McFarland 2015.
37. Vermeulen 2012, p.151.
38. "Cultural etiquette around the world" 2016.
39. Trotman 2014.
40. "A conversation with Temple Grandin" 2006.
41. Happé and Frith 2006.
42. Public Library of Science 2011.
43. Lorenz and Heinitz 2014.
44. Happé and Frith 2006.
45. Grandin 2009
46. Csikszentmihalyi 1990.
47. Bradberry 2014.
48. Blades 2016.
49. Gallup Inc 2006.
50. Zell, Warriner, and Albarracín 2012.
51. Goldstein and Naglieri 2013.
52. Kross *et al.* 2014.
53. Zell, Warriner, and Albarracin 2012.
54. Best *et al.* 2015.
55. Geller 2005.
56. Bogdashina 2016, pp.63–64.
57. Geller 2005.
58. Bogdashina 2016, p.124
59. Centers for Disease Control and Prevention 2016b.
60. Ludlow n.d..
61. American Friends of Tel Aviv University 2011.
62. Myles 2012.

INDEX